**NEA
SCHOOL RESTRUCTURING SERIES**

# Parents and Schools:
## From Visitors to Partners

E  D  I  T  O  R

## Rebecca Crawford Burns

*Robert M. McClure
NEA Mastery In Learning Consortium
NEA National Center for Innovation
Series Editor*

**nea** PROFESSIONAL LIBRARY

National Education Association
Washington, D.C.

# ACKNOWLEDGMENTS

I wish to acknowledge the contributions of several Appalachia Educational Laboratory staff members in the preparation of this manuscript: John R. Sanders, for his support of this effort; Robert Childers, for his support and encouragement, and his assistance with peer review; Patricia Penn, for her editorial perspectives; and Oralee Kieffer, for her invaluable secretarial skills.

I also wish to thank Robert McClure, NEA's *Restructuring Series* editor, for his confidence and patience in the completion of this work.

And I dedicate this book to the memory of my parents, my first and best teachers.

—Rebecca Crawford Burns

Copyright © 1993
National Education Association of the United States

Print History:
    First Printing:    October 1993

**Note**

The opinions expressed in this publication should not be construed as representing the policies of the National Education Association. Materials published by the NEA Professional Library are intended to be discussion documents for educators who are concerned with specialized interests of the profession.

### Library of Congress Cataloging-in-Publication Data

Parents and schools: from visitors to partners / editor, Rebecca Crawford Burns. p. cm.—(NEA school restructuring series) Includes bibliographical references (p. 90). ISBN 0-8106-1856-7 1. Home and school—United States. 2. Education—United States—Parent participation. I. Burns, Rebecca Crawford. II. Series. IN PROCESS                                                                                     93-31951 CIP

# CONTENTS

## THE ADVISORY PANEL

Nancy J. Abel, Fourth Grade Teacher, Greenbriar West Elementary School, Fairfax, Virginia.

Dorothy Rich, Founder/President of the Home and School Institute, author of *MegaSkills,* and developer of the MegaSkills Workshops Program.

Edna Henry Rivers, Guidance Counselor, W. P. Davidson High School, Mobile, Alabama.

Barbara R. Untch, Kindergarten Teacher, River Woods Elementary School, Naperville, Illinois.

# FOREWORD

Everyone connected with schools that are trying to improve their effectiveness knows that the key to real reform lies with parents and their engagement with their child's learning. Figuring out how to make that critical connection, though, has not been written about very much. This book breaks new ground on a critical subject.

As the reader will learn in the opening pages, the lessons shared here are from the real world of schools. Rebecca Burns and her colleagues have *talked* (if that is the right word for exchanges on an electronic network) with hundreds of practitioners and parents who have formed partnerships that work. These learnings are presented in a form that will help people in many different types of communities from the most privileged to those with the scarcest resources. And, as readers, we are permitted to visit two of the most interesting schools in the nation. Stewart Community School in Flint, Michigan, is alive with purpose, high standards, fine teaching, and the cause of much of that excellence—many, many parents. Mynderse Academy in Seneca Falls, New York, another place of vitality and terrific curriculum, is calling on its parents to play an important role in being advocates for excellence. We have much to learn from schools such as these that are leading the way in transforming public education.

The reader will also find a wonderful trove of resources here. There is an idea for every school willing to try a new way to, as Ms. Burns calls for, move parents from being visitors to full partners.

*—Robert McClure*
*Series Editor*
*Mastery in Learning Consortium*
*NEA National Center for Innovation*

# PREFACE

When I came to work at the Appalachia Educational Laboratory in January 1990, one of my first tasks was to learn to use the IBM computer on loan from the National Education Association so that I could begin my assignment as moderator of the Parent-Community Involvement Conference of the NEA School Renewal Network. I approached the task with fear and trepidation, never having used a computer and knowing nothing about the network. My job description as a conference moderator required that I build a data base of research on parent-community involvement in schools and facilitate conversation among Mastery in Learning (MIL) Project schools about their efforts to involve parents and community members in meaningful ways.

The support and encouragement I received from NEA staff and School Renewal Network participants was overwhelming. The responses to my papers on parent-community involvement, the stories about parent-involvement programs in the schools, and the technical assistance I received empowered me to enter information and queries online with confidence, and to respond to questions from the schools. It was this enabling, along with the instances of exemplary practice shared by the original MIL schools, that provided the foundation for this book. Without the information shared on the School Renewal Network by teachers, principals, and parents, this book would lack the richness of their perspectives and the wisdom of their experience.

This volume is built on the experiences of educators and parents who have put research into practice to improve children's learning. Inherent in the exemplary programs and practices described by the authors is the belief that parents must be engaged in their children's education, both in the school and in the home. The interdependence of educators and parents, their partnership of support for children, is the focus of this book.

The first chapter provides a review of the research on parent involvement, including its positive effects on children, families, teachers, and schools; the barriers to involving parents more actively in their children's education; and suggestions for overcoming the barriers. Chapters 2 and 3 focus on strategies for initiating and maintaining effective two-way communication between school and home, the key ingredient in school-home partnerships. Chapters 4, 5, and 6 provide in-depth descriptions of exemplary parent-involvement programs. Chapter 7 offers a summary of parent-involvement practices found in successful school programs. The book concludes with a list of resources from which educators and parents may draw as they plan, implement, and evaluate their partnership efforts.

Throughout the book, examples of successful practice, reflections of educators and parents, and the results of research are interwoven. The volume's primary purpose is to enrich the findings of notable studies of school-home partnerships and parent involvement with the experience and wisdom of those who have put theory into practice in homes and schools across the United States. It is the hope of the contributing authors that educators, parents, and others who read this book will find models for parent involvement that they can replicate or adapt to their needs, or reinforcement for the efforts they may already have underway.

—Rebecca Crawford Burns
Editor

Chapter 1

# PARENT INVOLVEMENT: PROMISES, PROBLEMS, AND SOLUTIONS

Rebecca Crawford Burns

> *Children in today's world need much more guidance and support from adults, and when they can see the adults in their lives as partners in positive ways, whether it's through conferences or parents stopping by or meeting casually with a teacher, those kinds of interactions are very powerful statements to children.*
>
> —Pat Green, Principal
> Columbia Park Elementary School
> Landover, Maryland

When school and family work together, a partnership of support for children develops. Education becomes a shared venture, characterized by mutual respect and trust in which the importance and influence of each partner is recognized. Although children, families, teachers, and schools benefit individually, their partnership enhances the entire process of education.

## THE PROMISES OF PARENT INVOLVEMENT

Research has demonstrated consistently that parent involvement is one of the keys to success in school for children of all ages and all types. Meaningful parent involvement results in improved student achievement, attendance, motivation, self-esteem, and behavior. Parent involvement also is a major contributor to children's positive attitude toward school and teachers. Indeed, the more parents are involved, the more children benefit (Henderson 1987).

9

Families, too, benefit from parent involvement. Studies have shown that participation in meaningful parent-involvement programs can improve parents' self-image, increase their respect for teachers and schools, and give them increased confidence in their ability to help their children succeed in school. For example, families participating in two projects, Cornell Family Matters and Cooperative Communication Between Home and School, became effective advocates on behalf of their children, became more involved in their children's education at home and in school, and generally became more productive members of their community (Cochran and Dean 1991).

When parents are involved, teachers gain an understanding of families' cultures, needs, goals, and capabilities. They also learn that parents can offer valuable resources, skills, talents, and creativity that can enrich teaching and learning. Through parent-involvement programs, teachers are able to share the responsibility of educating children with parents who can provide volunteer time, home help, and positive influences on their children.

Enhanced school climate is another consequence of constructive parent involvement. When schools reach out to involve parents, family attitudes toward the school become more positive. Positive family attitudes toward school in turn promote improved student behavior and school climate. James Comer's School Development Program illustrates the positive effects of school-home partnerships: parents become involved as educational decision makers, as links between classroom and community, as paid and volunteer school staff, and as implementers of academic and social programs (Comer and Haynes 1991).

## BARRIERS TO PARENTAL INVOLVEMENT

The benefits of school-home partnerships are evident, yet parental involvement in school programs and activities remains rare. Although teachers overwhelmingly agree that parent involvement contributes to student success, effective teaching,

10

and positive school climate, few teachers have strong parent-involvement programs in place (Epstein 1992). However, Comer (1988) discovered that parents want to know what is going on in the school, how the school system works, and how they can be a part of it. They also want to know what they can do at home to help their children succeed at school. If parents and teachers both consider parent involvement important, why isn't there more of it?

## Teacher Attitudes

> A lot of excuses can be given for not wanting parents in the classroom, but I have to believe that the real reason in most cases is the teachers' lack of belief in themselves (Clyde Collins, Teacher, Mynderse Academy, Seneca Falls, New York, NEA School Renewal Network, 1992).

Studies have identified a number of barriers that make it difficult for parents and teachers to work together. First, many teachers feel that parents do not have the time or interest to interact with them. For example, Davies (1989) found that many teachers believed that parents with low incomes did not value education highly or had little to offer to the education of their children. Teachers viewed these parents as "hard to reach," and cited poor social or economic conditions as the reasons. However, parents in this same study did not consider themselves hard to reach. Moreover, the school's parent-involvement practices were a more important indicator of the likelihood of parent involvement than was the socioeconomic status of parents.

> The data are clear that the school's practices to inform and to involve parents are more important than parent education, family size, marital status, and even grade level in determining whether inner-city parents get involved with their children's education in elementary school and stay involved through middle school (Epstein and Dauber 1989).

11

Despite the apparent benefits associated with parent involvement, the critical factors that predict the extent to which it occurs are the interest and initiative of individual teachers. Some parent involvement occurs because of parent initiative, but this is rare. Parents are interested, but they generally wait for direction and guidance from the teacher.

Reports of poor teacher attitude toward parent involvement generally focus on direct parent participation in the classroom. Some teachers are concerned that parents will encroach upon their areas of responsibility and will not follow instructions and school regulations, particularly in regard to confidentiality. They are afraid parents will cause confusion and disrupt the classroom. Others fear that parents may cause trouble if they see something in the classroom they don't like. These negative attitudes prevent teachers from engaging proactively with parents as partners in school.

*Parent Attitudes*

It's hard to define my role as a parent in the day-to-day operation (of school). I feel things are out of my realm and my participation as a parent isn't needed (Parent, NEA School Renewal Network, 1992).

Just as teachers have attitudes that hinder parent involvement, parents have attitudinal barriers as well. Many parents are distrustful of schools, or reluctant to get involved with them, because of bad memories from their own school days. Schools sometimes contribute to these negative responses by calling on parents only when their children have problems. If parents faced similar difficulties when they were in school, the negative feelings are reinforced. In addition, some parents view their child's performance as a reflection on themselves. To build trust and break down negative parent attitudes, teachers should get parents involved in special activities and school outings, enlist them as classroom or library aides, and incorporate them onto planning and management teams. Teachers should make a special effort to engage parents of disadvantaged students who stand to benefit the most from parent participation in their learning but whose parents are often reluctant to become involved. Comer's School Development Program demonstrates the significant role the family plays in creating a positive educational environment in both home and school. When the program was implemented in 1968, the two New Haven, Connecticut, pilot schools were suffering from severe achievement, attendance, and discipline problems. Parents were distrustful, alienated, angry, and dejected. By 1975, student behavior problems had declined, parent-teacher relations had improved, and the children's achievement levels had risen significantly (Comer 1988).

## Inadequate Skills

Even if they have positive attitudes toward the school, parents may not have the skills needed to help children learn and socialize. Perhaps one of the most important findings of the research, however, is that parents, regardless of education level, can and do make a positive contribution to their children's achievement in school if they receive adequate training and encouragement in the types of parent involvement that can make a difference (Cotton and Wikelund 1989). When teachers ask parents to help their children with schoolwork, parents usually respond more positively if they can do something that is comprehendible, fun, and likely to be successful. (See the discussion of the *Family Connections* model in Chapter 4.) Teachers should communicate to parents that their involvement and support make a great deal of difference, and that they need not be highly educated or have large amounts of free time for their involvement to be beneficial.

Unfortunately, many educators lack the necessary skills to work with parents. Indeed, many teachers and administrators are uncomfortable having parents in the school. Joy Adler, of Wells, Maine, (1992) a parent participant in the NEA School

13

Renewal Network, voiced her concerns on this issue:

> I love it when I attend a meeting and hear the speaker talking about educators and parents—or teachers and parents. Aren't parents educators? Aren't parents teachers? Boy, we keep hearing about kids who enter school not prepared! Parents weren't doing their jobs as first teachers! But once our kids are in school, we no longer seem to have a brain. Teachers are the professionals. We should leave them alone to do their job. I really had a teacher say that to me. My response was that she was the professional teacher and I was the professional parent. We each had a job to do. And the job of educating children was too big for either of us to do alone. Only by working together could we begin to solve the problems facing school.

Many parent-involvement programs are school-dominated, soliciting parent participation in activities such as fund-raising, bake sales, and chaperoning while not really encouraging meaningful involvement in other areas. Many teachers admit that they do not know how to involve parents in the classroom and still maintain their role as teacher, probably because they have not had the training and support needed to work with parents.

## Disparities Between Home and School Cultures

Differences between parents and teachers related to ethnicity, language, socioeconomic status, and education represent another barrier to school-home partnerships. When the educational environment is not sensitive to the home language and home culture, communication is difficult and parents may feel unwelcome at school and psychologically discouraged from initiating a dialogue with their children's teachers (Mannan and Blackwell 1992).

## Constraints on Parents' Availability

Increased demands on parents' time and changes in

family structure are also having an impact on parent involvement in schools. The proportion of women in the work force with children below age 18 rose from 40 percent to 65 percent between 1970 and 1988 (Mannan and Blackwell 1992). The number of single-parent families has also increased dramatically. Therefore, many families have limited time to devote to their children's education. Fewer parents are available during regular school hours to attend school activities, do volunteer work, or participate in parent-teacher conferences. These socioeconomic changes in the family affect the type and amount of parent involvement that is feasible in most schools.

> I think the key is to reach all parents to show them we care so much for their children. When we get the children so motivated to learn, to care, to share,... perhaps it may rub off on a few parents who need encouragement. Then they will share in our commitment to their children (Teacher, Tower Elementary School, Westerly, Rhode Island, NEA School Renewal Network, 1992).

## MAKING PARENTS PARTNERS: A FORMULA FOR SUCCESS

Parents and educators know what research has demonstrated: that parent involvement benefits children, parents, teachers, and schools. But knowing and doing are two different things. Successful school-home partnerships depend on at least three factors. They require: 1) committed leadership, 2) training for teachers and parents, and 3) a variety of involvement options for parents.

### Committed Leadership

*Committed leadership is crucial to effective parent involvement.* District and school administrators should establish parent involvement as a genuine schoolwide priority. Committed leadership for effective parent-involvement programs is characterized by these administrative supports (Wikelund 1990):

15

- written school and district policies that establish parent involvement as a legitimate and desirable activity
- clear and high expectations that parent involvement is a key to improved schools
- leadership and encouragement
- sufficient funding
- time allocated for staff to coordinate parent-involvement activities
- staff and parent training
- space and equipment
- food, transportation, and child care as needed for parent meetings.

## Staff and Parent Training

*Training for teachers should increase teachers' understanding of the community's culture, history, leadership, needs and concerns, and channels of communication.* Methods of developing open, two-way communication and personal outreach to all parents are essential as well. Also, teachers need to be aware of the various roles or options for parent involvement and determine which are most appropriate for their students. For example, the early childhood model of "parents as teachers," attending open houses, and coming into the classroom to volunteer may not be appropriate at the secondary level because of changes in the parent-child relationship and the teacher-student relationship. However, the continuing involvement of parents at the secondary level is important to student success. The exemplary parent-involvement program at Nashoba Regional High School, Bolton, Massachusetts, involves parents with teachers on committees that coordinate parent volunteers, develop programs on substance abuse, and organize fund-raising activities.

*Providing orientation and training for parents enhances the effectiveness of parent-involvement programs.* Research indicates that parents generally want and need direction. Orientation and training can take many forms, from providing written directions with a send-home instructional packet; to offering workshops where parents construct, see demonstrations of, and practice using instructional games; to presenting programs in which parents receive extensive training and ongoing supervision from school personnel, or participate as co-learners during inservice training (Cotton and Wikelund 1989).

Training for teachers and parents should define both teachers' and parents' roles and responsibilities and enhance their effectiveness as collaborators.

## *Variety of Parent Roles*

*When schools offer parents a variety of roles, parent involvement is most meaningful and successful.* Parents need to be able to choose from a continuum of activities that accommodate different schedules, preferences, and capabilities. Several researchers have defined types of parent involvement or parent roles. For example, the Southwest Educational Development Laboratory (1985) has identified three *traditional* and three *nontraditional* parent roles. *Traditional roles* include:

- *Audience:* Parents attend parent-teacher conferences and special school programs, fill out school information forms, and perform other basic obligations related to their children's education.
- *Home Tutor:* Parents help with homework, help children learn with material from home, and help children develop good study habits.
- *School-Program Supporter:* Parents go on field trips, help with the annual school play, help with fundraisers, and serve in other volunteer capacities at the school.

The traditional roles include those activities with which teachers and parents are most familiar and comfortable. The *nontraditional* roles are less common but are becoming more frequently discussed and experienced in schools. These include:

17

- *Co-learner:* Parents attend workshops and conferences with school staff, take part in staff-development activities, and attend educational activities for parents.
- *Advocate:* Parents take part in school-board meetings, speak at faculty meetings, initiate academic booster groups, and offer ideas to school and district administrators.
- *Decision Maker:* Parents help evaluate how well school programs work, help decide on school budget expenditures, and assist in the development of school and district policies and programs.

These six roles offer a smorgasbord of activities from which parents may choose. Each type of parent involvement yields some positive result, whether it be improvements in student performance, parent attitudes, or teacher competence. However, the greatest benefit results when schools enable parents to participate in a variety of roles over a period of time. In planning a comprehensive parent-involvement program, teachers and administrators need to assess their own readiness to involve parents and determine how they wish to engage them and put their capabilities to use. Further, they must communicate that parents are partners of the school and that their involvement is needed and valued. Together, teachers, administrators, and parents should develop short- and long-term goals and strategies for building home-school partnerships that support children's education.

I am looking forward to the day when it is "we," not "them and us"—when there is trust between administrators, teachers, parents, students, and community. I continue working hard and questioning; sometimes with success, sometimes getting "chewed out." But I believe strongly in the importance of parental involvement and continue to work to build trust and cooperation (Joy Adler, Parent, Wells, Maine, NEA School Renewal Network, 1992).

# REFERENCES

Cochran, M., and Dean, C. 1991. "Home-School Relations and the Empowerment Process." *The Elementary School Journal* 91 (1991): 264–69.

Comer, J. P. 1988. "Educating Poor Minority Children." *Scientific American* 259: 42–48.

Comer, J. P., and Haynes, N. M. 1991. "Parent Involvement in Schools: An Ecological Approach." *The Elementary School Journal* 91: 271–77.

Cotton, K., and Wikelund, K. R. 1989. "Parent Involvement in Education." *School Improvement Research Series,* Close-Up No. 6. Portland, Oreg.: Northwest Regional Educational Laboratory.

Davies, D. 1989. *Poor Parents, Teachers, and the Schools: Comments About Practice, Policy, and Research.* Paper presented at the annual meeting of the American Educational Research Association, San Francisco, March.

Epstein, J. L. 1992. *School and Family Partnerships* (Report No. 6). Baltimore: Johns Hopkins University, Center for Social Organization of Schools.

Epstein, J. L., and Dauber, S. 1989. *Teachers' Attitudes and Practices of Parent Involvement in Inner-City Elementary and Middle Schools* (Report No. 32). Baltimore: Johns Hopkins University, Center for Social Organization of Schools, March.

Henderson, A. T. 1987. *The Evidence Continues to Grow: Parent Involvement Improves Student Achievement.* Columbia, Md.: National Committee for Citizens in Education.

Mannan, G., and Blackwell, J. 1992. "Parent Involvement: Barriers and Opportunities." *The Urban League Review* 24: 219–26.

National Education Association School Renewal Network. 1992. Participants' comments. Unpublished network content.

Southwest Educational Development Laboratory. 1985. *Partnerships: Guidelines for Training Teachers in Parent Involvement Skills.* Austin, Tex.: Author.

Wikelund, K. R. 1990. *Schools and Communities Together: A Guide to Parent Involvement.* Portland, Oreg.: Northwest Regional Educational Laboratory.

Chapter 2

# COMMUNICATION: THE KEY TO EFFECTIVE PARTNERSHIPS

Oralie McAfee

> *Good communication between home and school is*
> *the key to parent involvement, and the key to good*
> *communication is an attitude that welcomes*
> *parents as peers in a context of mutual respect.*
> —*Susan McAllister Swap*
> *Institute for Responsive Education*

School-home partnerships depend on effective communication of the *right* messages. However, educators sometimes communicate the wrong messages: the school knows best; it is up to parents and children to conform; we are the professional educators. Parents, also, may convey the wrong message: that school efforts are inadequate or inappropriate. It is more difficult to communicate the right message: that the mutual respect and interdependence of home, school, and community are essential to children's development. Frequently, the problem lies in the *tone* of messages between school and home. Communication of positive attitudes may determine whether or not mutual support and useful interaction are established.

School personnel cannot abdicate their professional responsibility to lead, but they cannot succeed alone. The suggestions in this chapter are intended to help schools initiate and maintain effective communication: an essential—indeed, a key—aspect of partnerships with families and communities.

## FACTORS THAT INFLUENCE COMMUNICATION STRATEGIES

The things that make a school unique—its administrators and teachers, its students, and the values and expectations brought to it by parents and the community—also influence the way parents and school communicate. What works in a tiny rural school in Montana may differ from what works in a school in Chicago. An effective school-home communication strategy is based on assessment of several factors in the school community. These include:

- the desired outcome of improved communication
- the current status of communication with parents
- the ecology of the community
- student age and level of development
- the attitudes and skills of school personnel
- available resources.

## *The Desired Outcome of Communication*

Schools communicate with parents for many purposes: among others, to keep parents abreast of what's happening at school, to report on children's progress, to help parents do a better job of helping their children learn, to solicit parents' support, to involve parents in collaborative decision making, and to help parents meet their basic responsibilities. The purpose of the message from school influences the content and method of communicating. Reporting on a child's progress, for example, may or may not help parents assist that child with schoolwork. Empowering parents through participation in collaborative decision making may or may not influence the way they interact with their children at home. To be effective, communication must be targeted to achieve specific goals. It is not an end in itself.

Some states and school districts have policies that specify purposes for school-home communication. For example, California's policy calls for schools to provide information to parents on how to (1) foster their children's learning, (2) use community resources, (3) develop parenting skills, and (4) promote two-way communication between home and school (Chrispeels 1991). The legislation establishing Colorado's state-supported preschool

22

program mandates that schools provide parents with activities to do at home to help their children learn (Colorado Revised Statutes 1992).

When and for what purposes do you communicate with parents?

## Current Status of Communication

Schools and families vary as much in their communication patterns as they do in anything else. Some school communities have a high level of positive and open communication, trust, and confidence in each other as a result of established, effective communication patterns. In these communities, expanding or altering communication is not difficult. However, if effective communication has not been established, or if communication has deteriorated, and distrust, defensiveness, confrontation, or apathy is the norm, the task is infinitely more difficult. In other communities, established patterns of minimal communication that do not promote school-home partnerships exist. Teachers teach and care for youngsters in school, parents receive progress reports, and both parties are satisfied. They have staked out their territories. Each group remains separate from the other, and each perceives no need to change the communication pattern.

What is the status of communication in your school community?

## Ecology of the Community

The ecology of the community also influences school-home communication (Comer 1990). Rural communities generally have more personal, informal communication than urban communities because teachers and parents often live in the same locality. In urban areas, parents usually participate in formal groups such as parent advisory councils; communications from school likewise will probably be more formal (Gotts and Purnell

1987). In the ecology of the urban setting, schools may have to work harder to communicate at the personal level.

In communities where parents and children live within walking distance of the school, there are more opportunities for informal communication and for parent participation in the school. In a community where children are transported by school bus, teachers may see parents less frequently, and may need to look for other ways to reach them. For example, at Lassiter Middle School, Louisville, Kentucky, a large percentage of the students live some distance from the school. Many parents do not own automobiles, and public transportation does not connect their homes with the school. To overcome this barrier to parent participation, the staff at Lassiter initiated an outreach program that takes them into less-accessible areas for regular visits and conferences (Virginia Heckel, Lassiter Middle School, Louisville, Kentucky, NEA School Renewal Network, 1992).

A stable community presents communication options and challenges that are different from those in a community marked by population turnover and structural instability. Social conditions such as poverty, violence, substance abuse, lack of adult supervision, and deteriorating family and community stability can make even basic communication seem an over-whelming challenge to school staff and parents (Edwards and Jones Young 1992).

Schools should consider single-parent homes, blended families, and other "nontraditional" child-rearing arrangements in planning communication. Children in blended families may have different last names; some married women choose not to change their last names; many grandparents are caring for their grandchildren. Before telephoning, making a home visit, or sending a written communication, school personnel should check parents' and pupils' last names and attempt to determine how parent and child are related. In some cases, schools may have to make progress reports, including the results of conferences, available to two sets of parents.

24

Schools must take into account diversity in cultural, racial, and ethnic background; the languages spoken in the community; levels of income, education, and employment; the quality and quantity of local housing; and other demographic and social characteristics of the community. For example, there is little need to install a voice-mail system if few homes have telephones. If many families speak a language other than English, communication from the school should be in that language as well as in English. When both parents are working, parents and schools will need to make extra efforts to establish and maintain good communication, regardless of all other factors.

The ecology of the community need not be a barrier to effective communication, as Epstein (1987) dramatically illustrated in her study of teachers' abilities to involve single parents as teachers of their school-age children. However, school personnel may need to adjust their ways of interacting with parents in order to establish and maintain productive communication.

What community characteristics affect your school or district plan for school-home communication?

## Student Age and Level of Development

As children mature, both the nature and the form of school-home communications change. "Happy-grams" of the preschool and primary years give way to notes or other forms of communication appropriate for older children. However, no approach should be dismissed too quickly. For example, home visits are usually made only to households with preschool and kindergarten children, and few school personnel at any level make regular telephone calls to parents. Yet these two approaches were combined with other modifications in a successful high school dropout prevention strategy. A visitor went to the homes of all dropouts and potential dropouts to work with parents and students to promote persistence in school. For junior high and elementary students identified as potential dropouts, volunteers

25

made "care calls" each time a student was absent from school. These strategies, combined with referrals to appropriate community agencies, were remarkably effective in reducing the dropout rate (Marockie and Jones 1987).

Parents of children at the preschool and elementary levels traditionally have been more receptive to parent education, but many schools are finding that parents of adolescents are seeking similar assistance. In Hawkins County, Tennessee, the school system offers parenting programs to parents of preschoolers, elementary-age children, and teenagers. Each program helps parents acquire communication, listening, and discipline skills needed for effective parenting of children in the designated age group (Gwinn 1991).

How does your school adjust its communication strategies as children grow and develop?

## Attitudes and Skills of School Personnel

Not all school personnel are equally comfortable interacting with parents. Some are defensive, philosophically convinced that school and learning have little to do with the home, while others are unwilling or unable to muster the time and energy needed to extend school-home communication beyond a required minimum. Many, however, involve parents as partners in a variety of ways, tailoring what they do to reach and communicate with particular families (Vandegrift and Greene 1992).

Most school personnel need training and support to enhance their communication abilities. One school principal was dismayed that it took her so long to realize that the collaborative decision-making body at her school was having difficulties, not with the content of its deliberations, but with communication and conflict-resolution skills.

Secretaries, bus drivers, custodians, aides, and other support staff can make or break lines of communication with parents and the community. In many districts, bus drivers talk with parents more often than teachers do. The warmth and friendliness of the person who answers the telephone and meets people at the front desk can set the tone of communication for an entire school. Specific guidelines for appropriate behavior, along with training in human relations and communication skills, will help *all* staff become part of a supportive communication link with parents.

Schools that provide an inviting "parent space" in the lobby, offer "family resource centers," or serve as "family resource schools"—working closely with or even housing community services such as health clinics, recreation, extended day care, and adult education—have a unique opportunity and challenge to communicate a "welcome" that school personnel can build on. In such situations, opportunities for informal communication greatly increase, but so does the potential for miscommunication. For all the good they will bring, partnerships and collaborations among schools, families, and communities will not diminish the need for constant attention to communication.

What attitudes and skills help or hinder your school's efforts to involve parents?

## Available Resources

Many communication strategies call for commitments of time and money that may not always be available. The costs of newsletters, parent-education materials, mileage for home visits, school-home liaisons, electronic equipment for hot lines and voice mail, and reimbursement for school personnel who work after hours may be prohibitive. However, resources are available to the creative educator determined to support school-home communication. Many schools establish partnerships with local businesses, corporations, foundations, and other groups to help defray communication costs. For instance, local television and radio stations often sponsor and publicize homework hot lines and parenting "helplines." In Vermont, a "Parentlink" voice-

27

mail system is part of a 10-year plan of school assistance developed by the Vermont Business Partnership. Elsewhere, private companies help schools with fund-raising activities. To implement voice messaging in one elementary school, teachers paid for their individual voice-mail boxes, while the school and the parent organization covered other leasing costs.

Other schools collaborate with community groups and agencies to complement and extend their communication with parents. For example, Kentucky has established family resource centers in selected schools.

What community resources are available to support and extend school-home communication in your school or district?

## GUIDELINES FOR EFFECTIVE COMMUNICATION

The first step in establishing an effective communication process is to analyze school and community factors that affect that process. Once this information is obtained, school personnel should develop and maintain a plan for regular communication with parents. Following are some tips and guidelines for doing this.

1. *Develop and publicize a regular, reliable communication process.* If educators don't know what information parents and the community expect or find helpful, and how they want to receive it, they should *ask.* Schools may have one thing in mind, while parents may want something else (Vandegrift and Greene 1992). Successful school-home communication begins where parents are—their interests, needs, and capabilities—not where the school might wish them to be. School communities might start by organizing work groups composed of staff and parents; consulting with the parent advisory council or school-based management team; conducting a survey of parents, community members, and staff; and reading literature on the types of communication most

helpful to parents. Regardless of the methods or content, school-home communication should:

- be timely. Newsletters and notices should allow enough lead time for parents to respond (Gotts and Purnell 1987). Voice mail should give this week's or today's messages, not last week's.
- provide for both personal and general messages. Personal messages pertain to an individual child. General messages apply to a group, such as the fifth grade at Island View School, all students at Midvale High, or parents and pupils in District 52.
- emphasize the positive. However, they should also discuss problems clearly and forthrightly.
- give parents the information they need. Perhaps because schools have worked with so many parents and children, they may assume that procedures and necessary responses are "obvious." But each year brings a new wave of children and parents, to whom everything may be new and nothing may be obvious.
- provide substantive information on children's progress: what they are learning, how they are learning, and how parents can help.
- be clear, concise, and free of jargon.

2. *Increase the potential for two-way communication.* Most methods of encouraging two-way communication are quite simple. For example:
   - Put the school's name, address, and telephone number on all communications, including releases to the media. When appropriate, add "For more information, call (write, see) _____ at _____."
   - Provide a list of important numbers for parents to post by the telephone or program for speed dialing. Among others, these might include the school's main number, absence line, homework hot line, and voice-mail extensions. Be prepared to respond. If parents are

29

asked to notify the school of their child's impending absence, make sure the absence line is open or that a message service stands ready to receive early-morning calls.

- Tell parents how to get in touch with and work with their child's teachers, principal, guidance counselor, and other relevant school staff. Suggest topics and concerns to discuss and state the times school personnel are available for telephone calls or conferences. Principals and teachers should not be "too busy" to meet with parents.

- Listen actively and reflectively during face-to-face and telephone communications. Let parents know you hear and understand what they say. If you and the parent speak different languages, locate someone who can translate and who can help with any other cultural differences.

- Include as part of the communication process a procedure that calls for a parent response or sign-off. For example, ask parents to comment on and sign samples of student work, notes from the teacher, or announcements of upcoming school or class events.

- To facilitate a quick response, ask parents to use their first and last names when leaving messages on voice mail or with school personnel, or when sending notes to school. School personnel should also use first and last names when communicating with parents.

- Use parent surveys, focus groups, or forums to sound out parents and community members on matters of concern or anticipated major changes in school policies or activities. Surveys provide an opportunity for the entire school community to respond, not just the "squeaky wheels."

- Use information gathered from parents in a constructive way. For example, publicize parent survey results as well as what school personnel will do in response to the findings. If parents provide assessment informa-tion, use that information to help their child.

3. *Employ a variety of communication strategies.* One group of parents and teachers compiled more than 300 pages of communication ideas and strategies to help school personnel involve parents at both the district and the classroom levels (Chrispeels, Boruta, and Daugherty 1988). The ideas—and variations and additions—that local schools can supply will likely fit any situation. Combinations of the approaches listed below, when used with a particular school community or family, will enhance communication. The suggestions are neither exhaustive nor new, but give some idea of the range of options.

   - Conduct surveys, inventories, or meetings soliciting parents' suggestions, ideas, opinions, and preferences to help school personnel and schools be sensitive and responsive to the community. Plan parent and family activities to match the needs and interests of the families and communities involved. Exhibit and display students' work to show what they have studied and learned. Involve parents in budget discussions to help everyone understand fiscal realities and set priorities. Discuss family and community concerns that intrude upon school learning to communicate to everyone ways to create a learning community.
   - Get the word out. Supply information for local television, radio, and newspaper stories or "spots." Have school representatives field questions on local interview or call-in shows, not just about homework or classroom studies, but about parenting and other community concerns. Make special efforts to provide information in media that reach particular cultural, ethnic, or language groups. Make presentations available to local community groups and organizations. Conduct some activities away from the school, in

31

places parents may feel more at home; such outreach says more than words ever can. Make videotapes and audiocassettes of school meetings, classroom activities, presentations, and other school functions available to parents who are unable to attend.

- Involve parents in school activities as classroom assistants, library assistants, specialized resources, "experts," and in other volunteer capacities. Such involvement provides an excellent opportunity for increased communication and understanding from both teacher and parent perspectives. Acknowledge and honor such participation, even the most tentative and hesitant. Involve parents as full partners on site-based management and collaborative decision-making teams, where everyone has to improve communication skills!

- Use newsletters, calendars, brochures, and leaflets to suggest parent-child activities that directly reinforce school learning as well as provide information to enrich family life and learning. Epstein (1987) suggests that this form of parent communication and involvement provides the biggest payoff for student learning. If children are having problems, list some specific things parents might do to help. If broader life skills or "megaskills" are needed such as getting organized, taking responsibility, setting priorities, and managing time, activities designed to accomplish these goals are readily available (Rich 1988).

4. *Make full use of options to enhance individual and personal communications.* Seemingly simple tools should not be overlooked in the effort to enhance communication with parents at the one-to-one level.

- The most powerful communications take place face to face and voice to voice. "Something as simple as a friendly conversation with the classroom teacher can go a long way toward building parent support" (Vandegrift and Greene 1992). Visit families in their homes and in community settings. Make personal telephone calls. Schedule regular parent and parent-pupil-teacher conferences. Allow pupils to explain portfolios, journals, displays, and other work to parents. Send personal notes or letters and encourage parents to share information in the same way.

- Develop procedures to take advantage of "drop-off" and "pickup" times at schools where parents provide transportation. Those few minutes are often very productive, especially when children are young enough that parents come into the school.
- Take advantage of the easy, informal communication that can flower when parents are in the school building regularly, as they are in family resource schools and centers, or with an extensive parent-volunteer program.
- Use school-home communication folders: a folder for each child to carry messages and work back and forth from school and home daily or weekly. Provide a place for personal messages from teachers to families and from families to teachers.

## CONCLUSION

Closer cooperation and mutual support among schools, families, and communities are essential to meet the challenges confronting education. Better communication of the right messages is central to that cooperation and support. Communication methods appropriate for helping schools and families become partners in education are within our reach. What we must do now is use them to reach out to each other, with whatever means are available and appropriate. Only through mutual respect, support, and interdependence can schools, parents, and communities create an environment that promotes learning for all children.

## REFERENCES

Chrispeels, J. H. 1991. "District Leadership in Parent Involvement: Policies and Actions in San Diego." *Phi Delta Kappan* 72: 367–71.

Chrispeels, J., Boruta, M., and Daugherty, M. 1988. *Communicating with Parents.* San Diego, Calif.: San Diego County Office of Education.

Colorado Revised Statutes 22-28-101 et seq, 1992.

Comer, J. P. 1990. "Home, School, and Academic Learning." In *Access to Knowledge: An Agenda for Our Nation's Schools,* edited by J. I. Goodlad and P. Keating. New York: College Entrance Examination Board.

Edwards, P. A., and Jones Young, L. S. 1992. "Beyond Parents: Family, Community, and School Involvement." *Phi Delta Kappan* 74: 72–80.

Epstein, J. 1987. "Parent Involvement: What Research Says to Administrators." *Education and Urban Society* (special issue on school-family relations, edited by R. F. Purnell and E. E. Gotts) 19: 119–36.

Gotts, E. E., and Purnell, R. F. 1987. "Practicing School-Family Relations in Urban Settings." *Education and Urban Society* (special issue on school-family relations, edited by R. F. Purnell and E. E. Gotts) 19: 212–18.

Gwinn, T. S. 1991. "Positive Parenting." *Focus on Instruction* (supplement to *The LINK,* February issue) Vol. 10 #4.

Marockie, H., and Jones, H. L. 1987. "Reducing Dropout Rates Through Home-School Communication." *Education and Urban Society* (special issue on school-family relations, edited by R. F. Purnell and E. E. Gotts) 19: 200–05.

National Education Association School Renewal Network. 1992. Participants' comments. Unpublished network content.

Rich, D. 1988. *MegaSkills: How Families Can Help Children Succeed in School and Beyond.* Boston: Houghton Mifflin.

Vandegrift, J. A., and Greene, A. J. 1992. "Rethinking Parent Involvement." *Educational Leadership* 50: 57–59.

Chapter 3

# THE POTENTIAL OF COMMUNICATIONS TECHNOLOGY

Oralie McAfee

> *I hope we learn how to talk to each other in languages we understand. Once we can communicate, we can develop the vision for telecommunications technology in K–12 education.*
> —*Dr. Robert R. Rath*
> *Northwest Regional Educational Laboratory*

The power of communications technology is dramatically illustrated in popular culture and political life, as talk-show hosts, instant telephone polls on current issues, satellite linkups for national "town meetings," and toll-free numbers shape public opinion and action. No one would wish for schools to be saddled with instant judgments based on video and audio persuasion, but we must recognize the power, pervasiveness, and utility of modern communication technology and learn to use it constructively. Indeed, technology played an important role in the preparation of this chapter. School Renewal Network requests for grassroots experiences and recommendations resulted in a wealth of information. Telephone access allowed analysis of a broad sampling of teachers' messages to homes. Computer searches of appropriate data bases located relevant information in minutes.

Electronic communications technology holds the promise of increasing and enhancing communication between home and school. Schools are just beginning to experiment with linkages such as voice mail and voice messaging. Like all other forms of communication, their effectiveness depends on the conscientiousness, skill, and attitudes of the people using them.

## HOT LINES AND HELPLINES

Homework hot lines or helplines, crisis lines, dial-a-teacher, parenting helplines or warmlines, Ed Info, Talk Box, and other dial-in systems depend on families to initiate calls. Some supply homework help, provided by trained volunteers or paid staff, directly to pupils. In Indianapolis, the television homework hot line has a call-in format, with teachers showing parents and children how to solve mathematics problems. Dial-a-teacher and parenting helplines have a broader function of helping families with parenting or school-related concerns. In some cases, trained volunteers discuss with families a wide range of concerns related to children, learning, and schools, and make referrals when needed. Others offer a "menu" of recorded messages related to children and learning, similar to what many hospitals offer through Tel-Med and other call-in information lines. Some simply change the recorded message and parents hear whatever is on. For example, Omaha, Nebraska's Chapter 1 Talk Box focuses on topics related to books and reading (D'Angelo and Adler 1991).

## AUTOMATED CALLING

Automated calling allows a school or district to call a particular group of parents to deliver a specific message, prerecorded by an administrator, specialist, teacher, or support-staff member. The system is programmed to call between set hours—say, 5 p.m. and 9 p.m. on weeknights. It keeps calling until all parents are reached or the shutoff hour arrives. Automated calling originally was developed to notify the parents of students in junior and senior high school when a child had an unexcused absence from school or class. Creative administrators and teachers now use targeted calling to convey all types of information, especially to inform and remind families of parent meetings, workshops, and learning opportunities. For example:

College Night will be Tuesday, November 1 at 7:30 p.m. in the North Bay Gymnasium. All students and parents at North Bay High are invited to attend to get information to help them make plans for the future. Representatives and information from many colleges and vocational schools will be available to answer your questions.

Effective? One principal's chagrin at the drop in attendance when someone accidentally neglected to have the computer notify parents of a meeting was more convincing to him than controlled studies and statistical significance.

## VOICE MAIL AND VOICE MESSAGING

Voice mail and voice messaging are the latest technological contributions to school-home communications. Messages are recorded and left in "mail boxes" that can be accessed 24 hours a day, seven days a week, by anyone with a touch-tone telephone or an adapter for a rotary phone. There is a direct voice connection between sender and recipient. Schools, parents, and teachers may know these systems under names such as Class Notes, Parent-Teacher Intercom, and ParentLink. This discussion focuses on the school-family communication aspect of these systems' primary functions: administration and instruction. As many schools began to automate selected administrative and secretarial functions as a means of cutting personnel costs, they found added benefits. With a telephone call made at their convenience, families can get up-to-date information on school events and activities, practices, meetings, parent conferences, lunch menus, and almost anything else of interest. School closings or schedule changes because of severe weather or other emergencies can be put on the system immediately, allowing families time to plan. Families can leave word of a child's absence at any time of day or night, or leave a request for a conference with a principal, specialist, teacher, or counselor. Messages from families are sent electronically to the appropriate person or entered into the records.

Voice mailboxes for teachers, specialists, and counselors are used primarily in support of instruction. Each teacher or team has an extension number that is made available to students and families, who may call from anywhere at any time to receive a two-to-five-minute recorded message. They listen as many times as they need to, and leave a message in the teacher's mailbox if they wish. Callers can always reach a "real" person during school hours if they want information beyond what is on the recording.

Most systems monitor the times a given number is called, the number of messages left, the dates and number of times the outgoing message was updated, the duration of the announcement, and almost anything else that can be tracked by computer. Administrators usually receive a monthly report as well as a cumulative reports by extension number and by school. Schools may decide to purchase or rent voice-mail systems. Voice-mail systems that do not require capital outlay from schools are available in most urban and suburban areas. Companies that rent or lease voice-mail services have their own central system through which calls are routed, so school telephone lines—and capital-outlay budgets—can be freed up for other purposes. Schools that purchase or lease to own complete voice-mail systems should make sure they are prepared to maintain the system and accommodate the changes that inevitably accompany emerging technology.

## What Can Voice Mail Do for School-Home Communications?

The only sure effect of voice mail on school-home communications is that communication will increase. NEA School Renewal Network data collected in 1992 from a survey of parents and teachers from 20 Vermont schools using ParentLink, a direct voice-mail system, showed that:

- Voice mail got heavy use. More than 86 percent of parents and 90 percent of teachers used the system; more than half of the parents contacted the school through ParentLink more than once a week; 15

percent of the parents used the system at least once a day.

- The 14 percent of the parents who did not use the system at all either had other means of school-home communication, did not have the right type of telephone, didn't understand how to use the system, or simply didn't want to use it.
- The system required little additional teacher time. Three-fourths of the teachers took less than 15 minutes to update a message.
- Parents, teachers, and principals had a positive view of the voice-mail system. Eighty-seven percent of the parents and 75 percent of the teachers thought it was a good idea. More than 77 percent of the parents thought that the presence of voice mail improved their child's school, and 65 percent of the teachers thought so. Principals thought voice mail fostered parental involvement and would recommend it to similar schools.

Although the evidence from Vermont is impressive, voice mail's capacity to make a difference in school-home relations or in student learning remains to be determined.

*Promise and Problems*

Like any other communication method, voice mail has its promise and its problems. Properly used, it can promote a public perception that a school is responsive and accessible. Families can find out what they need to know about what's going on in school and have a direct link between themselves and their children's teachers. Some teachers become skillful at establishing rapport with families as they use voice mail to communicate expectations and suggestions. When families use voice mail, the feelings and concerns behind the words are communicated to the teacher. When parents or guardians leave detailed questions or messages,

39

the teacher, specialist, or counselor can be prepared for a productive telephone conference when he or she calls back.

*Voice-mail links with the home establish that pupils, parents, teachers, and specialists are all in the educational enterprise together.* Teachers can suggest things parents can do at home to help their children. Children and parents can check to make sure homework and other assignments are clearly understood. Children who are absent can get their assignments and keep up—a real time-saver for teachers. Once a voice-mail system is implemented, the excuse that "I didn't know I was supposed to do that" should become a thing of the past. Some teachers file a written script or detailed outline of each message, so they have a evidence of the "opportunity to find out."

*A voice mail/messaging system can raise the level of school and teacher professionalism.* Most business and service organizations install systems of this type to make full use of professional time and to make sure messages don't get lost on their way to the mailbox. Unfortunately, few teachers have telephones in their classrooms or work areas, but voice-mail systems enable them to enter, change, or retrieve messages from any touch-tone phone at any time. Itinerant teachers and specialists, who often have no desk or home school, can use voice mail as a way of establishing communication with parents.

*Voice mail/messaging can be adapted to any age or grade level; student grouping or administrative unit; or subject, content, or developmental area.* Although most people think first of homework or assignments, the content of voice-mail messages is limited only by the ingenuity of the teacher. Motivation to use the system can be built in, with a question, assignment, or riddle of the week, "secret message," extra credit, prize for the twenty-fifth parent to leave a message, or other enticements to get children and families to call. One fourth grade teacher in Colorado reported that even though he didn't install the week's message until Sunday evening, many children had the answer to the question of the week when they came to school Monday morning.

Teachers may be unwilling to use this system because it requires that they plan ahead in order to give an overview of upcoming work. They also must be consistent in updating messages and returning calls. If they are not, the family's (or anyone else's) image of both teacher and school will suffer, and even the most conscientious student or parent will quit calling. Plus, hurried, perfunctory messages are heard and interpreted in just that way.

Other shortfalls include the fact that some teachers and parents have a philosophical objection to anything automated; others are afraid of the technical aspects of voice mail, or even of using the telephone as a recording device.

Language can sometimes be a barrier as well. However, if students' families do not speak English, "press zero" can be used to connect them with someone who speaks their language. Voice messaging can handle only a limited number of languages, though.

### How Schools Can Maximize the Potential and Help Overcome The Problems of Voice Mail/Messaging

Several procedures can be used to maximize teachers' acceptance and effective use of voice mail.

- Install a voice-mail system that requires teacher participation only after adequate study, explanation, demonstration, involvement, and commitment from the entire school community: administrators, teachers, parents, pupils, governing board, and teachers' organizations. Some school personnel may resent the system's ability to monitor and measure use, how and when messages are updated, and other aspects of their work. They may not like the fact that anyone can check on their assignments and messages. Such feelings need to be discussed upfront.
- Head off potential problems before they arise. If there is to be one voice mailbox per team of teachers, how

41

will responsibilities be delegated? Teachers may worry about responding to an overload of parent messages. While some schools may get many messages, getting parents to *leave* messages may be a challenge at other schools. Make sure to agree on limits ahead of time, such as not picking up messages over the weekend.

- Assign the first voice mailboxes to teachers who volunteer for them, or at least make some allowances for individual preference. One teacher refused to use the voice-mail system, but worked out a compromise with her principal by agreeing to take calls at home during specified hours each week.

- Provide staff training, not only on technical matters but on content, delivery (many messages are delivered too fast for the listener to keep track of dates, page numbers, and other important information), ways to build teacher and family motivation to use the system, time-savers, and generally on how to achieve the full potential of the system. Message frameworks will help teachers who have trouble deciding what to say. For example:

Hello, this is Dee Maestes, extension 1295. The week of March 3rd we'll be studying.... Students, you'll be responsible for.... Parents, here are some things you can do at home to help.... The question of the week is.... If you need more information or have questions, leave a message. Be sure to leave your name, number, and the best times for me to return your call.

- Allow time for teachers, parents, and children to learn how to use the system. Provide motivation for everyone, not just the children. If necessary, educate families to use the system to help their children, and include guidance on appropriate messages to leave for teachers.

- Experiment with the possibilities. There are no

"rules." Could capable older students or volunteers record some messages? Would a standard weekend message be helpful, something like, "Call in for the next message on Monday afternoon after 2:30; have a nice weekend"? Experiment with time intervals between messages. Perhaps a short message every day would be easiest and most effective. Perhaps longer intervals correlated with school learning are more appropriate.

- As everyone becomes more experienced, share message ideas among teachers and teams to maintain motivation and interest and to keep the messages fresh and interesting.

## How Teachers Can Use Voice Mail to Connect School and Home

Once voice mail has become an accepted tool among teachers, there are many specific ways teachers can use it to foster connections between school and home.

- Give overviews of projected work and expected learning, linking them to what children have learned earlier and will be learning later.
- Specify assignments, including due dates, specific pages, projects, methods ("We'll be working in the library on Monday and Tuesday"), spelling words, and any related explanations. Explain items to be done at home and how parents can help: "We're doing a project on mollusks, and your children will need to go to a market that sells clams, oysters, or other mollusks to find some of the information. They know what they're supposed to do, but would appreciate your help."
- Review homework assignments, providing tips to parents on what they can do to help, or tips for children to assist them over rough spots.

- Remind children and families of deadlines and opportunities: "Send field-trip permissions before Friday." "We'll be classifying grasses on Thursday, May 4th, so bring your examples before that time." "An author/storyteller will be visiting our class on Monday afternoon, October 19th. Parents, you will enjoy this, too. If you can go, leave me a message so I can arrange seating. If you can't go, ask your child to share the experience with you."
- Supply information about field trips: the purpose, what to wear, food requirements, and so on.
- Briefly explain a school emphasis, such as alternative assessment, emergent reading and writing, critical thinking, problem solving, or cooperative learning, and provide suggestions to parents for what they can do to reinforce related objectives at home.
- Use voice mail for student assessment. One foreign language teacher has students call in, introduce themselves, request something, or reply to something she has said on voice mail. She then listens to each student's individual use of the language.
- Suggest learning opportunities for families: good television programs and movies, a television program related to what children are learning, free and low-cost community resources and events, related books and resources at the public library, natural phenomena specific to a given community. If parents don't know how to use these resources, give some suggestions appropriate to the age of the child.
- Leave messages "for adults only." Of course the children will listen, but that's all right! For example, discuss upcoming parent conferences, and give parents the opportunity to leave their questions and concerns in the mailbox so you can be prepared. Acknowledge and thank parent volunteers (and solicit more). Give a "parenting tip of the week," or an inspirational or

humorous "thought for parents." These might be more beneficial than a list of assignments, and would be appropriate to leave on a weekend or holiday. We have all said to ourselves, "I wish every parent in the school could read or hear that." With voice mail they can.

- Discuss any general problems, suggesting what parents can do to help, or soliciting their suggestions. For example, if young children have trouble getting themselves to school with the items they need, suggest things that parents can do at home to help them get organized. Pass on tips from other parents.
- Convey a personal "signature" or philosophy. One teacher ends all his voice-mail messages by directly exhorting students to "study hard."

## CONCLUSION

The potential of communications technology remains largely untapped by schools. However, it holds great promise for linking school and homes. The use of communications technology to form partnerships with parents is limited only by the commitment and creativity of school personnel.

## REFERENCES

D'Angelo, D. A., and Adler, C. R. 1991. "Chapter I: A Catalyst for Improving Parent Involvement." *Phi Delta Kappan* 72: 350–54.

Macro International. 1992. Cited in *The Condition of Education 1992: Making Changes, Measuring Results*. Montpelier, Vt.: Vermont Department of Education.

National Education Association School Renewal Network. 1992. Participants' comments. Unpublished network content.

Chapter 4

# PARENTS AS FIRST TEACHERS: "THE FAMILY CONNECTIONS" MODEL

Patricia Penn and Robert D. Childers

> *The most important educational influences in my*
> *life were undoubtedly my parents.*
> *—Robert Root Bernstein*

A review of research on effective early childhood programs reveals one essential component: meaningful parent involvement. We now know that *what* children learn as preschoolers may not be as important as parental involvement in the process. Evidence that parents want what is best for their children, and want to help them learn, is clear and abundant. Anne Henderson's (1987) annotated bibliography on how parent involvement improves student achievement describes 49 studies that back this up.

It's one thing to tell parents that they are their children's first and most important teachers, but it's quite another to make them comfortable with the idea. After all, most of us grow up with the idea that a teacher has to have special skills and knowledge. Many parents want to do everything they possibly can to help their children succeed in school, but not many believe they know what to do. What the Appalachia Educational Laboratory (AEL) in Charleston, West Virginia, has demonstrated with a product called *Family Connections* is that when families are provided with materials that are inexpensive and easy to use, they will happily work with their young children to help them learn.

## WHAT IS "FAMILY CONNECTIONS?"

*Family Connections* is a set of 30 four-page guides that

AEL developed to help teachers and others provide opportunities for parents and children to have fun doing things together that suit a child's stage of development. The guides are sent serially, with one arriving each week. The guides include:

- a message to parents, covering such topics as the importance of reading aloud, of using effective discipline strategies, using the public library, and learning through play. The messages, like everything else in *Family Connections,* are written at the fifth grade level or lower to ensure that most adults will be able to read and comprehend them.
- one or more read-aloud selections, such as nursery rhymes and original verses, intended to stimulate imagination and make language fun. Not all homes have books and magazines at hand, so every issue includes something to read aloud.
- developmentally appropriate activities for parents and other family members to do with their young children. The activities use materials commonly found in homes and require little preparation by parents. Each issue includes original art and illustrations.
- a "Sunshine Gram" in the second issue and every fourth issue thereafter. The Sunshine Gram gives teachers and others an opportunity to have a positive communication with families on a regular basis. Many parents learn early that a message from school is apt to be bad news; the Sunshine Grams are intended to teach a different lesson.

## CHARACTERISTICS OF "FAMILY CONNECTIONS"

The research on which the *Family Connections* guides are based goes back more than two decades to AEL's Home-Oriented Preschool Education Program (HOPE). HOPE identified a base of 59 competencies that are part of physical, emotional, social, and cognitive development in children. A panel of 34 early childhood practitioners created guidelines to be used in preparing parent-child activities to develop those competencies. All were tried successfully with children in Head Start and other preschool programs, and in kindergarten. Teachers from 14 states tested the original activities, which use materials relevant to children's own life experiences. *Family Connections* staff revised and updated many of those original activities for the current guides, which were pilot tested in 1992 in 10 schools in five Kentucky districts.

Each issue of *Family Connections* has a space for the child's name so the guides can be personalized. As teachers and other users put a name on each guide, they can think of how something in that issue might be helpful to a particular child. Educators can identify home activities in *Family Connections* that might suit a child's particular needs and call the parent's attention to them. Teachers can further personalize the guides by addressing the Sunshine Gram in each issue to a child's parents or to the child himself or herself.

The guides need not be used sequentially. They are numbered for user convenience, but can be used in varying order. Because the first issue includes a brief description of the guides and a message to parents about their being the first and most important teachers of their children, it logically would be best to use it first. Teachers can then use the guides in any order. For example, they might find that a particular issue fits with a unit they are planning and decide to send that issue home the week of the unit, or the following week, to reinforce learning. The guides are not seasonal, so they can be started at any time during the year, and used year-round. Users can develop their own inserts to send home in *Family Connections*. For example, if a teacher is having a parent meeting, an announcement about it could be put into the guide. The program provides camera-ready headers for a number of inserts, including such titles as "This Week in the Classroom," "We're Going on a Field Trip," and "Special Announcement."

*Family Connections* is designed to reinforce both dimensions of developmental appropriateness: age and individual differences. Activities are based on the belief that what children learn during the early years should help them make sense of their own experiences.

In deference to the strong likelihood that not every parent will want to do everything in an issue every week, activities are varied so that something in each issue will appeal to different tastes and interests. Activities and illustrations are also designed to be sensitive to the range of configurations that families take today. Both text and illustrations are intended to foster families' awareness of America's rich cultural diversity. Also, gender roles are not depicted stereotypically. For example, little girls are shown playing with trucks, and little boys are shown working in the kitchen.

## REACTIONS FROM PARENTS AND TEACHERS

Determining if parents were using *Family Connections* was a major concern during field-testing. One of the "gaps" in research that Henderson enumerated in the 1987 bibliography was in the types of resources parents and educators need if they are to work effectively as partners. AEL wanted to help close that gap, and was particularly interested in parents' evaluation of usability. The pilot teachers sought parent reaction as part of the research, using a form AEL provided (Childers and Penn 1992). Most decided to get reaction more frequently than required by data-collection needs because they found it useful in their own planning for use of the guides. The pilot teachers also thought it was a self-esteem builder for parents to be asked for their opinions. Teachers also validated parent use with remarks children made when teachers used material from the guides in class: "I know this poem. Daddy read it to me last night." "We did opposites when I got home yesterday."

One teacher who was involved in the field test characterized the guides with one word: *easy.* "A busy parent can pick this up and spend five minutes with a child and achieve so much. It's easy to work with, and it gives you new ways to use old things. Some of our families use it with kids at church; some even use it on car trips. They love it," the teacher said. "In the classroom, I have observed that some of the shy children have really responded better since they've been taking *Family Connections* home. I think it's because their parents have been spending more time with them and encouraging them to talk more. Sometimes a child will come up to me and say, 'I know a poem,' and when I hear it, it will turn out to be something from *Family Connections*."

Another teacher, responding to an external evaluation some months after the field test (Evaluation Center 1993), noted that use of the guides "provided a concrete link between the home and school. During home visits, many parents commented on the enjoyment shared by the parents and child while using *Family Connections*." Another said using the guides "helped us to better communicate with families and created a team effort to help the children learn and grow." Another said that using the guides as a way to involve parents in the schooling of their children "strengthens collaboration between children, parents, and school!"

A Head Start teacher who was part of the field test related that all the parents who had a child returning to the program asked if they would be receiving *Family Connections*.

Other teacher reactions included these:

- "Many parents want to give their preschooler a good start, but they don't know where to start. The *Family Connections* newsletter was there every week to give them direction and creative ideas."
- "The parents said it put good ideas at their fingertips. They are busy, but could do these activities."
- "*Family Connections* is great to send home to get the parents involved. Parents like to keep them and use them again at different times of the year."

Parents responded enthusiastically to the guides, too (Burns 1992). Some of their reactions:

- "Rhymes increased my son's memory power."
- "My child loves to be read to, so he enjoyed stories and poems."
- "The front-page message to parents provided answers to questions I had. It was encouraging to know that I wasn't the only one with these questions."
- "The stories, nursery rhymes, and illustrations were at my child's level and easy to understand."
- "The activities were easy to do and my child liked them."
- "My daughter wanted me to sit down and read to her as soon as she brought the guide home from school."
- "I got ideas from the activities that I could adapt to make up new ones of my own."
- "The newsletter helped me teach my child things I wanted to teach her but had been unable to. She listened better with *Family Connections.*"
- "The materials are really educational, plus they help develop a bond with your child."

## IMPLEMENTING "FAMILY CONNECTIONS"

*Family Connections* project staff considered what might get in the way of parents using the guides: Parents are busy people. Single parents especially have more than enough to do. Some parents are intimidated by schools and teachers. Others think that schools should do the teaching. A few parents can't read, or read poorly.

But parents want what is good for their children. They are eager to help when they know what to do. The field-test experience with *Family Connections* was that most families eagerly welcomed the guides, and teachers took steps to create and

51

maintain this interest (a handbook including suggestions and techniques is included with each package of 25 sets of the guides).

For schools interested in letting their community know about this parent-involvement vehicle, AEL provides a news release in the handbook that can be easily localized; field-test schools that used it got good coverage. *Family Connections* guides do not have to go into homes through schools. One innovative coordinator of family programs introduced the guides at parent workshops. Parents who wanted to use them with their children signed a request form. The guides are mailed to them.

A home visitor can take the guides into homes. In some Head Start programs, family educators are using *Family Connections* with parents and children together. Some family educators provide materials for the activities; for example, one program bought inexpensive magnifying glasses for the children to use.

## CONCLUSION

*Family Connections* guides first became available for the 1992–93 school year. Within six months they had been ordered by programs in 15 states. Kentucky, where the guides were field-tested, ordered 20,000 sets to be used in programs for at-risk four-year-olds statewide. A second volume of *Family Connections,* geared to children of kindergarten age and older, was scheduled to be available for the 1993–94 school year. The Rural Excel Program, which produces the guides, is exploring the possibility of producing Spanish-language versions.

To obtain a brochure on *Family Connections* and a free sample issue, write to *Family Connections* at AEL, P.O. Box 1348, Charleston, WV 25325.

## REFERENCES

Burns, R. 1992. *Parent Reactions to "Family Connections," Volume I: A Follow-up Study.* Charleston, W.Va.: Appalachia Educational Laboratory.

Childers, R. D., and Penn, P. 1992. *Field Test Evaluation of "Family Connections," Volume I.* Charleston, W.Va.: Appalachia Educational Laboratory.

Epstein, J. 1987. "Effects on Student Achievement of Teachers' Practices of Parental Involvement." In *Literacy Through Family, Community, and School Interaction,* edited by S. Silvern. Greenwich, Conn.: JAI.

Epstein, J. 1984. Improving American Education: Roles for Parents. Testimony before the Select Committee on Children, Youth, and Families, U.S. House of Representatives, June.

Evaluation Center (Western Michigan University). 1993. *FY 92 Report of the External Evaluation of the Appalachia Educational Laboratory.* Kalamazoo, Mich.: Author.

Henderson, A. 1987. *The Evidence Continues to Grow: Parent Involvement Improves Student Education.* Columbia, Md.: National Committee for Citizens in Education.

Gotts, E. E. 1980. "Long-Term Effects of a Home-Oriented Preschool Program." *Childhood Education* 56: 228–34.

Chapter 5

# MYNDERSE ACADEMY: PARENTS AS CO-DECISION MAKERS AND ADVOCATES

Clyde Collins

> *When parents are involved, children do better in*
> *school, and they go to better schools.*
> *—Anne T. Henderson*
> *Author of The Evidence Continues to Grow*

Change is a journey, not a destination. At Mynderse Academy, the journey began in 1987 with the school's participation in the National Education Association's Mastery in Learning (MIL) Project. This involvement led us to a venture in shared decision making in which the principal and a core of teachers began to imagine a different type of schooling—one that gave parents a greater voice in their children's education. Although the effort to involve parents in governance at Mynderse Academy succeeded, parents and staff experienced frustration and struggled to overcome obstacles along the way.

Steering-committee members are still building trust and working to improve decision-making skills. Also, committee members sometimes experience frustration at the hesitancy of some of the faculty and most of the community to consider real comprehensive restructuring rather than a piecemeal approach. This chapter describes committee members' efforts to affect change and charts the progress made in the journey toward greater parent participation at Mynderse.

# SCHOOL PROFILE

## Demographic

Mynderse Academy is a public school that serves grades nine through 12 and is located in the Finger Lakes region (Seneca Falls, to be exact) of upstate New York. The township of Seneca Falls has a population of about 75,000, with another thousand people in the outlying areas being served by the district. The population is almost entirely Caucasian. Employment has been on the decline in this town. There is only one major employer, Goulds Pumps, an international company; its corporate offices and foundry are located in Seneca Falls. The majority of Goulds's employees are blue-collar workers, but there is a fairly large middle-management group. Socioeconomically, Mynderse students generally represent the middle class.

The student population averages about 100 students per grade. Mynderse students share a building with local middle school students (grades six through eight); each group is taught in different halves of the same building. Student crossover is highly limited; some staff, however, teach at both levels. Restructuring in the middle school has been a result of its metamorphosis from a junior high. Unfortunately, because of the necessity for cross-teaching, the schedule of the middle school has remained synchronized with that of the high school, which remains traditional in both organization and method of instruction.

## Barriers to Parent Involvement

Neither school has a traditional parent-teacher organization, although the middle school does have parents who volunteer at school activities such as dances and fund-raisers. The local school district does not have a history of welcoming community involvement. For example, when the school board conducts its open meetings, public participation is limited to "comments," and major decisions are often made in closed "executive sessions." Because the traditional top-down hierarchy has remained firmly in place in the district, parent involvement at Mynderse historically has not been enthusiastic. Attempts to form parent-teacher organizations have been unsuccessful, even though about 40 percent of the families attend school open houses.

## Groundwork for Change

Changing parents from infrequent, voiceless visitors to full partners in school decision-making at Mynderse was facilitated by two events: (1) the school's participation in the NEA's Mastery in Learning (MIL) Project, which involved faculty in shared decision making; and (2) a 1990 mandate from the New York State Board of Education that required each district to include teachers and community members in school restructuring efforts. Although the faculty at Mynderse had initiated site-based management during its participation in the MIL Project, top-down management was still firmly in place at the district level. It was this tension between the central office and building personnel that precipitated greater parent involvement at Mynderse.

Despite the state mandate for faculty and community involvement in decision making, the district superintendent created building-level steering committees composed of the building principal plus a group that was two-thirds parents and one-third teachers. Because of their size, both Mynderse and its feeder middle school were to have 30-member committees. Membership was voluntary on a first-come basis, and parent participants were required to have a child in their respective committee's school. All those volunteering to serve on the steering committee were subject to approval by the school board.

Because they had participated in shared decision making and developed a school plan to involve parents in restructuring efforts, most of the Mynderse faculty refused to participate in the superintendent's plan for a top-down steering committee. During the next few months, teachers met with parents who had volunteered to serve on the Mynderse steering committee. These parents also agreed not to participate unless each building was permitted to establish its own requirements for committee participation and organization without school board approval. Eventually, the superintendent agreed to these terms.

## PARENTS AS PARTNERS IN DECISION MAKING

Empowered by their ownership of the steering-committee structure, parents and teachers quickly rallied against any encroachment on their decision-making autonomy. Both groups were willing to volunteer time and effort only if they were the decision makers on building issues other than the hiring and firing of school personnel.

Although steering-committee members and faculty agreed to maintain a 30-member limit for the committee as outlined by the superintendent, they decided to permit 50-percent staff representation rather than the original 2:1 ratio of parents to teachers. Currently, the committee is attempting to make its membership more reflective of the community. For example, community representatives who are not parents can now serve on the steering committee, and parents need not live in the school district in order to serve. The latter provision permitted separated parents to participate in school decision-making. Students could now serve on subcommittees, but they could not yet be voting members of the steering committee. These changes are increasing parent and community involvement at Mynderse and improving school-home communication. The steering committee meets monthly. Meetings are cochaired, usually by a parent and a teacher, on a rotating basis to ensure that eventually every member has a chance to serve. The principal has not chaired the committee since its first meeting. Because committee decisions are made by consensus, most new members attend summer workshops on group decision-making and consensus-building strategies to enhance their work on the steering committee.

Staff and parents are proud of the steering committee's accomplishments. Each spring, the committee administers the New York State Effective Schools Consortia Survey to all staff, parents, and students. The survey is mailed to parents with a cover letter, and students complete the survey during extended homeroom periods. Students are asked to encourage their parents to return the completed survey, which could be hand-delivered by the student in an unmarked envelope to ensure anonymity. Each year, 40 percent to 50 percent of the parents have responded to the survey. During the summer, a subcommittee analyzes results of this needs assessment and drafts a school action plan for the coming year based on survey data. The plan is reviewed, revised, and approved by consensus vote of the entire faculty in the fall. After staff approval, the plan is again presented to the steering committee for further review and final approval. The fact that there has been little disagreement between the faculty and the steering committee is testimony to the committee's accurate interpretation of survey data and awareness of faculty needs. During the year, staff and parents implement the action plan.

## PARENTS AS ADVOCATES

The action plan encourages parent involvement with education at school and at home. For example, monitoring student progress is a concern of many parents. In response to this concern, staff now contact parents more frequently regarding students' progress, sending more than 1300 "reports" yearly for a student body of approximately 450 students, in addition to issuing regular report cards and phoning students' homes. Teachers also conduct monthly grade-level meetings to discuss students' progress. If three or more teachers feel that a student is not working to potential, a staff member would call the parents; frequently, the result would be the scheduling of a parent conference. In 1992, staff and a representative group of parents evaluated the school's conference and open house procedures. As a result of the evaluation, the school began holding two open houses; the first is a get-acquainted session during September and the second is conducted six weeks later after mailing of the first formal notification of student progress. The later open house is dedicated primarily to parent-teacher conferences. Currently, a subcommittee of the steering committee is investigating ways to get parents more involved in monitoring homework.

The steering committee is actively involved in other areas of school improvement. For instance, it's investigating the issue of "creating a climate of expectation that students can reach an extended level of achievement." This includes defining exit outcomes for all students that go beyond course credits and completion of curricular assignments. The steering committee also has authorized a pilot plan for portfolio assessment.

After studying relevant research and visiting other schools, the steering committee recommended that staff increase detracking efforts and offer more heterogeneously grouped courses. In response, heterogeneous grouping started to be used in some English, social studies, and science classes.

Other examples of parent and community involvement at Mynderse include: (1) an expanded career day, which brought businesspeople into the school to "show and tell" with the students; and (2) "career shadowing," an activity in which students followed and observed businesspeople at their jobs.

## OUTCOMES OF PARENT INVOLVEMENT

The involvement of parents on the building steering-committee created a two-way flow of communication that improved parent and staff understanding of each other's unique problems and concerns. Most parents, when asked, professed a desire to "better understand the structure of schooling in Seneca Falls" and "to work with teachers to make the daily educational process more productive." This second objective is particularly significant, given that many parent members of the steering committee were working mothers who expressed concern over seeing young people enter the work force with weak writing skills, little motivation, and a tendency to lack pride in doing a good job.

In an informal survey, parent members of the steering committee were asked to express their views, both positive and negative, about their experience on the building steering-committee. The following are representative responses:

- "I would rate our current process as fairly effective. I feel a sense of empowerment, but (I also feel) that I really have to work for it."
- "We spend a lot of time talking about doing things, but we need to actually *do* more."
- "I feel that we (parents and teachers) are really working as a team. Even though we don't always understand all the problems, the principal and teachers are very patient about explaining all the obstacles to just doing something differently. There never seems to be time or money to do anything different from what we are doing."
- "I like the idea of consensus instead of voting, but it is very time-consuming. It forces us to be more honest with each other and more willing to compromise."
- "I think that we (parents) have changed some things because of our participation, but we seem to be only affecting those things that have no money strings attached to them."
- "There has to be a payoff for any committee member, be it parent or teacher. Otherwise it becomes just another meeting and people won't come out. The individual has to feel that (he or she is) making a difference."
- "Our committee seems to have just 'friends of the school.' Do we need to actively seek out a broader community representation?"

The successful operation of the Mynderse steering

committee influenced change at the district and state levels. New York state law now mandates a district-wide steering committee composed of one teacher, one parent, and the principal from each building steering-committee; the district superintendent; and five additional community representatives who do not serve on building committees. The district steering-committee, which meets three times yearly, is not empowered to make decisions that affect individual schools; rather, its purpose is to coordinate building-level efforts when necessary and to serve as an information clearing house. This function, which supports building steering-committee efforts while preserving committee's autonomy to make decisions, is viewed positively by most, but not all, participants on these committees.

Community members of the district committee who do not serve on a building committee express surprise and sometimes dismay at the decentralization of decision-making power. One member remarked: "This seems backwards. How will we get them to do what we want if we don't have the authority to tell them to do it?" For many, the old paradigm is still firmly in place.

However, the district steering committee has affected positive change. For example, Goulds Pumps, Seneca Falls' major industry, funded a districtwide benchmarking plan for educational improvement. The initial project was "technology in education," and grant monies from Goulds were targeted to support related training and travel expenses for school staff, with individual building-committee approval. The company also offered to work with school staff and steering committees "to fuse the industrial concept of 'quality' with educational realities." District steering-committee members soon afterward began to take training in this process.

## A LOOK TOWARD THE FUTURE

Unless we can change the whole structure of education, we can only tweak and twiddle. There is a growing frustration on the part of parents and teachers that inertia will prevent meaningful changes. In Seneca Falls, parents gained a better understanding of how the economics of schooling had been the primary factor in creating and maintaining the existing structure. As a first step toward making decisions about how money is allocated and spent in the district, some parents and teachers plan to become experts on the school budget. This would be a major step toward empowering the building steering-committee to make informed decisions about the budget and toward increasing their understanding of the domino effect of those decisions. New monies for restructuring seemed unlikely; therefore, reallocation of existing funds would be necessary to affect change.

However, implementing and maintaining change does not depend solely on economics. True restructuring requires new knowledge and skills and a new vision of schooling. In many instances, reconceptualizing education means discarding sacred cows such as lectures and standardized tests for more collaborative instructional strategies and more telling methods of evaluating teaching and learning. Making these changes is not easy. Staff, parents, and community must understand the rationale for change and be committed to research-based educational improvement. At Mynderse, the steering committee initiated this process during the 1992-93 school year by evaluating its progress toward fostering and managing meaningful change and using the NEA School Renewal Network data base as its primary source of information.

Although the effort to get parents involved in governance at Mynderse Academy was a success, it will take time for the lines of division between community and school to become blurred. We told ourselves at the onset of this educational revolution of the 1990s that it would probably take the rest of the decade to make meaningful changes. Therefore, educators and parents need to be patient with each other and to continue to believe that the walls obstructing our progress will crumble if we keep hammering away at them.

Chapter 6

# STEWART COMMUNITY SCHOOL: A PIONEER IN HOME-SCHOOL PARTNERSHIP

Robert R. Simmons, Barbara A. Stevenson, and Ann M. Strnad

> *It takes a village to raise a child.*
> —*African Folk Saying*

Yo participo.
Usted participa.
Ello participa.
Nosotros participamos.
Usted participa....Ellos aprovechan.

I participate.
You participate.
He participates.
We participate.
You participate....They profit.

There is a critical difference between going through the empty ritual of involvement and having the real empowerment to affect the outcome of the processes. This difference is capsulized in the above quotation. The quotation highlights the fundamental point that involvement without empowerment is an empty and frustrating process for the underrepresented parents. It allows the school to claim that all stakeholders (parents, teachers, administrators, community members) were considered, but makes it possible for only some of those stakeholders to benefit. It maintains the *status quo* (Arnstain 1969).

In many American cities, there is a growing understanding that schools alone cannot handle the task of educating children who have a wide array of needs. Schools need the collective support and assistance of parents and the community. Schools need to be partners with the community so that children come to school healthy and ready to learn. Staff and parents at Stewart Community School have found that the most effective way to achieve their shared goals for children is to work together.

This chapter is the result of almost three years' work using the National Education Association School Renewal Network data base and information contributed by Mastery in Learning (MIL) Project schools that have active, successful parent-involvement programs. The chapter describes programs at Stewart Community School in Flint, Michigan, that have enhanced parent involvement and student performance.

## DEFINITION OF PARENT INVOLVEMENT

The term *parent involvement* is used broadly in this chapter and includes several different forms of parent participation. The authors' definition of parent involvement is compatible with the Flint Board of Education's definition of community participation:

> The Flint Community Schools will encourage and provide opportunities for students, faculty, and other members of the community to interact through open channels of communication in order that they may play an effective role in the planning, development, implementation, and evaluation of the school program (Flint Board of Education 1987).

Flint's definition of community participation emphasizes the city's commitment to the concept of community education as a *process* throughout the school district and community.

At Stewart Community School, all parent-involvement activities focus on the following outcomes:

- Parents will be taught and encouraged to be actively involved in their children's education.

64

- Parents and teachers will have consistent communication as part of a strong partnership of adults working in support of a child.
- Parents and community members will have educational opportunities, linked to the goals of the school, in parenting, mentoring, and teaching/learning.
- All children, especially children who do not have strong parent models or support, will have a community-based mentoring program.
- Parents will be actively involved in the decision-making and governance structure of the school.

## SCHOOL PROFILE

The Flint School District is widely recognized as having one of the oldest and most successful community-education programs in the United States. Although the program is more than 50 years old, the district recently made sweeping changes in order to restructure its community programs. Today, each school in the Flint district has a Community Advisory Council (Stewart's is called "As One") consisting of the principal, home-school counselor, community education "agents," program assistants, teachers, and other community members. This system brings together community residents and school staff to identify and solve school and community problems as well as promote projects to improve the school and the community. Citizen and parent participation through the Community Advisory Council is an important feature of the community education program in Flint.

### Demographics

Located in a large urban district, Stewart Community School has 496 students, prekindergarten through sixth grade. Stewart serves an increasingly diverse student population in a geographic area marked by sharp changes in its social structure and demographic patterns since the early 1970s. Seventy-six percent of the students enrolled at Stewart are from single-parent families, a dramatic increase over past years. Ninety-six percent of Stewart's students are African-American; 2 percent are Caucasian and 2 percent are Hispanic. Approximately 53 percent of the students receive free or reduced-price lunches. The school population "turns over" at an annual rate of 19 percent.

Changes in the external environment have paralleled often-significant alterations in achievement rates and student discipline. Students seem minimally skilled or, in some cases, entirely unskilled at conflict management and interpersonal relations. Detention, in-school suspensions, behavioral contracts, and formally closed classes serve as stop-gap measures rather than as permanent solutions to perennial discipline problems. These factors suggest that traditional educational programs have not meaningfully addressed student achievement and other related facets of the school program. They further suggest that, like the community, students at Stewart are experiencing dynamic change.

To meet the diverse needs of the school community, Stewart staff members have initiated a number of efforts to provide quality education for the children and adults they serve. These programs reflect the need to involve parents and community in school improvement, and the positive results of such involvement for children and adults.

### Barriers to Parent Involvement

More often than not, barriers exist that impede the parent-involvement process. These barriers may be actual or perceived by staff, students, or parents, and exist in many schools. At Stewart, parents, staff, and students have cited barriers to parent involvement, and staff and community have developed programs to overcome these barriers and create a better learning environment for all involved. Parent/community involvement activities now focus attention on several factors that have limited parental involvement at Stewart in the past: (1) parents' negative feelings about school, based on past experiences; (2) feelings of alienation resulting from previous interactions with school staff; (3) a lack of opportunities for meaningful involvement; (4) the need for transportation; and (5) insufficient support and direction for various forms of involvement.

The key strategies for building stronger community support were developed through the following process.

1. developing a vision
2. establishing a written plan
3. soliciting community participation
4. informing the community
5. coordinating school and community activities
6. soliciting feedback from the community.

The following goals for school improvement were targeted by staff, parents, and community members.

- *Academic Skills:* Students will improve in reading and mathematical thinking, science, speaking, and writing by demonstrating skills appropriate to their grade level.
- *Social Skills:* Students will demonstrate appropriate social skills to maximize development of self-direction, self-esteem, and personal responsibility.
- *Home/School/Community Relations:* Students will benefit from the involvement of parents and the business/community partnership.

## PARENTS AS DECISION MAKERS

### School Improvement Team

To implement the school improvement goals, the Stewart School Improvement Team (Steering Committee) was initiated during the 1986–87 school year under the NEA Mastery In Learning Project. The School Improvement Team

(SIT), an outgrowth of the Steering Committee, was designed during the 1989–90 school year to meet the Flint Community School Board's goal of having 10 schools develop a site-based management/shared–decision-making model that would encourage all faculty, parents, and community members to be a part of the problem-solving process.

Stewart's School Improvement Team meets a minimum of once per month. The SIT is composed of a maximum of two members representing the administrative staff, the union (teachers and paraprofessionals), support and custodial staff, and a maximum of three parents from the community. Each group elects its own representatives, and efforts are made to include all segments of the staff and community.

Responsibilities of the SIT include decision making and problem solving in areas such as:

- access to learning
- identifying, obtaining, and allocating instructional resources
- assessing progress toward school goals
- facilitating communication among internal as well as external groups
- determining policies concerning visitors and information dissemination
- reviewing budgets.

Because of time constraints, all concerns must be brought before the SIT. The SIT listens to concerns on any issue, from any individual or group, and refers these concerns to the appropriate committee.

Ad hoc committees provide a means of bringing any other proposals to staff meetings for discussion. Under the Stewart governance model, there are five standing committees: the Parent, Budget, Curriculum, Climate, and Enrichment committees.

The functions of the Parent Committee are to:

- increase the number of parents involved in the education of their children
- encourage improved achievement
- motivate students to do their best
- increase participation on committees by parent and other community members
- evaluate programs.

The functions of the Budget Committee are to:

- order, organize, and distribute supplies
- budget allocated funds
- investigate alternative funding.

The functions of the Curriculum Committee are to:
- pursue development of alternative curriculum
- suggest instructional procedures to ensure student success
- study test results to determine strengths and weaknesses
- help plan and implement staff development.

The responsibilities of the Climate Committee include:

- Clean-Up Day
- retirement and transfer functions
- Parent Recognition Day
- open house refreshments
- supervision of hall guards, patrol boys and girls, and flag students
- coffee hours
- flowers and cards sent on occasions of illness and death.

The responsibilities of the Enrichment Committee include:

- honors programs
- enrichment programs
- career programs
- programs on diverse cultures.

Committees submit their proposals and recommendations to the SIT, which then determines the agenda for staff meetings based on recommendations from the committees. After each committee's presentation, the staff reaches a decision by consensus, if possible. If consensus is not possible, a vote may be requested by a staff member. A two-thirds majority is needed for approval of a decision. If such a majority vote cannot be attained and time does not permit further discussion, the proposal may be sent back to the committee with which it originated.

## *As One*

In 1990, Stewart parents organized "As One," a parent-community committee that assists with decision making. A member of the group attends all school committee meetings and reports back to "As One." Carol Shearer, an "As One" leader, described the group's goals and activities online for participants in the NEA School Renewal Network:

> As One's intention is for parents and community to become one with the school. We hope to establish a home-learning center at Stewart that will be operated and supervised by As One, using materials to assist children in learning new skills or in troubled (academic) areas. We also hope to train parents in preparing their children for school and keeping them interested in school. Training in conflict management, reaching consensus, and how to organize and conduct a meeting are also on our agenda. We are pursuing business partnerships so that we all can become "As One" (NEA School Renewal Network 1991).

Many activities have been initiated by As One. The group submitted a proposal to the Charles Stewart Mott Foundation and received $750 to purchase diverse cultural materials and to provide cultural programs for students, staff, and parents. As One also organized and implemented a Christmas card sale. Students drew holiday scenes, and parents selected four of their entries to be printed on the cards, which were then packaged and sold. Funds raised by As One have been used primarily to establish a home-learning center at the school.

Parents and other community members are involved in school-based decision making at Stewart through their participation in committees, SIT, and staff meetings. They also play other roles that support the school.

## PARENTS AS TEACHERS

Parents want their children to succeed in school and frequently ask, "How can I help; what can I do?" At Stewart, programs developed for and with parents offer advice and specific suggestions on (1) what parents can do at home to improve students' academic achievement; (2) what parents can do at school to improve students' academic achievement; and (3) what parents can do to reduce the types of student behavior that undermine the teacher's ability to teach and the students' ability to learn.

Each year, parents of children from six months of age through grade six are invited to attend a workshop at the school. Using prepared booklets and bulletins, teachers and parents provide suggestions on how to help children at home. For example, during the workshop, parent responsibilities in regard to homework and home reading are defined. After the workshop, parent, student, and teacher develop a reading/language contract.

Based on the findings of a questionnaire completed by teachers, parents are asked to assist in classrooms in a variety of ways. Parent volunteer activities include:

- using prepared vocabulary flash cards, phrase cards, and math flash cards with small groups of children
- helping one to four students who missed words on

spelling tests

- assembling homework papers to take home
- checking and posting the names of students returning daily homework
- monitoring students after school who need to finish work, were late to school, or "fooled around"
- listening to children read to gain fluency.

Parents who attend workshops receive incentives such as storybooks, vocabulary-card files, and school supplies. Parents who volunteer to assist at school also are recognized with appropriate awards.

Stewart staff ask each parent to establish a routine at home that prepares the young child for the routine required at school. In addition, parents are asked to assist students at school with lavatory and hallway passage; and during scheduled movement to the library, gym, and lunchroom.

To evaluate the effects of increased parent involvement, the SIT monitors grades, attendance records, and disciplinary referrals. Parent involvement and staff effectiveness are evaluated through surveys, questionnaires, informal interviews, and examination of records. For example, staff formulated a pre/post questionnaire for parents designed to identify the extent of parent involvement at home. Records of parent participation at school were charted to determine the number of parents involved.

Following are one parent's reflections on her experience with parent involvement at Stewart.

My involvement as a parent began when my first child started kindergarten. My husband and I decided that I would stay home with our children. It was very difficult to think that my young five-year-old daughter would now be in the hands of strangers who would have an everlasting impact on her life. When I met my child's first teacher, I must say it was refreshing. She was kind and patient; this eased the fear I was experiencing. Later, I discovered my child's class was larger than I thought a kindergarten class should be. This made me question the attention each child would receive. I knew I had prepared my child well for school, but I was worried about all of the other children who may not have a parent home with them or a parent to spend the quality time I was able to give my child. I informed my child's teacher that at any time she needed help with any thing at all, to please ask. And she did! She wanted her classroom, ultimately, all classrooms in the school, to have computer exposure. That was the beginning of my formal parent involvement. This gave me the opportunity to meet the entire staff at our school, most of whom I found to be quite compassionate. Due to the fact I did not work outside the home, I had time to do a little more. I became interested in class assignments, extracurricular activities, and the structure/operation of the building. By the end of my first year and after many questions to the teachers, support staff, and principal, I became much more aware of the politics involved in educating my child (NEA School Renewal Network 1992).

In theory, everyone agrees that involvement of parents and the community is good for the children and the school. But what level of participation is sought by the school or offered by the community? Schools often say they want or have a good level of parent participation, but in actuality, do they? Does the level of involvement get beyond volunteering? Do parents really influence and participate in the decisions made at the school level in cooperation with staff?

## PARENTS AS CO-LEARNERS

Survey data collected by the As One parent group indicated parent interest in a computer class. After a business partnership was established between Stewart School and Electronic Data Systems (EDS), EDS donated 15 computers to the school. EDS personnel also volunteered their time and expertise to offer computer classes before and after school for both students and staff. Because parents also wanted to learn to use computers and the EDS instructor was not available during the school day,

73

a Stewart teacher agreed to offer two classes at set times. Following are the teacher's reflections upon completion of those classes.

A Teacher's Idle Thoughts...

For two weeks I taught a computer class for the parents of Stewart School students. I must admit that I was reluctant at first, because proper preparation was needed, and I didn't know if I could pull it off by Monday. The parents who came were generally people who had never turned on a computer before. I know that I overwhelmed them with computerese on Monday, but I knew things would be okay when on Tuesday they were back and raring to go. We learned word processing, and within a couple days parents were editing, using spell check, moving blocks of text, underlining, boldfacing, and so on. The delight that I saw on their faces was extremely satisfying.

I thoroughly enjoyed my two weeks. I was particularly proud when one of the parents told me that she gained the confidence to check into going to a local college, qualified for grant monies, and enrolled in computer classes. Now that's success! (NEA School Renewal Network 1992).

Although Chapter 1 programs traditionally have a parent-involvement component, Stewart School offers extended parent-education opportunities for Chapter 1 parents. The Chapter 1 Social Service Field Worker (SSFW) serves as a liaison between the home and the school. In this role, the SSFW organizes and maintains a building-level Parent Advisory Council (PAC). The collective councils form a citywide PAC. This council is essential to the planning, implementation, and evaluation of the district's Chapter 1 program. Research indicates that children whose parents are positively involved in school activities tend to be more successful in school. To this end, the Stewart PAC provides training for parents on various topics, such as positive discipline, learning styles, AIDS awareness, health education, and career options. The success of these training sessions becomes evident when parents move from involvement to parent education. A successful transition becomes apparent when parents assume leadership roles, such as serving as presenters and classroom volunteers, with confidence and competence.

## PARENT INVOLVEMENT: THE PAYOFF

Increased parent involvement at Stewart has produced a number of positive results. For example:

- Parents have greater knowledge of child development and parenting skills.
- Increased interaction between home and school fosters understanding of and support for the role of education in career choices.
- Workshops in academic areas help parents to assist their children with homework.
- A shared partnership between parents and school staff increases parents' self-esteem and leads to improved student academic achievement and attendance.

Clearly, it is imperative that parents be involved in the education of their children. As one Stewart School parent said, "When the staff is there with us making decisions, we feel we are all working together." Another parent said, "We must learn that it takes both of us, the teacher and the parent, to successfully educate a child. Both school and home learn from each other."

The principal and staff at Stewart concur that parent involvement is essential. We need parents who are comfortable in schools and knowledgeable about the process of schooling. We must empower parents to take their rightful place along with teachers and administrators in providing a meaningful education for their children, for without parents, there can be no effective schools and no effective education for the children who need it most.

Parents, community, and staff at Stewart School strive to work together, and the children reap the benefits of this collaboration.

> I participate.
> You participate.
> He participates.
> We participate.
> You participate....All profit.

## REFERENCES

Arnstain, S. 1969. "A Ladder of Citizen Participation." *Journal of the American Institute of Planners* 35: 216–24.

Flint Board of Education. 1989. *Flint Community School Strategic Plan, 1989–1994*. Flint, Mich.: Author.

National Education Association School Renewal Network. 1991, 1992. Participants' comments. Unpublished network content.

Chapter 7

# FROM VISITORS TO PARTNERS: A SUMMARY OF EFFECTIVE PARENT-INVOLVEMENT PRACTICES

Barbara A. Fleming

> *Lasting school improvement will prevail only if we, as educators, pursue and encourage parent involvement and get "Beyond the Bake Sale."*
> —*Lawrence W. Lezotte*
> *In his foreword to Beyond the Bake Sale*

For many years, schools and families understood themselves as having separate and distinct roles in children's lives. Children were expected to learn the three Rs at school, and the home was responsible for children's physical well-being and for instilling values such as "doing your best." Schools had little reason to interact with families on a regular basis. As long as schools did their job (teaching), and families did their job (nurturing), everything went fairly smoothly. The school was thought to know what was "best" for children educationally and provided parents with limited information. Most interactions between school and home were social events such as open houses.

Under this paradigm of school-home relationships, the flow of information was limited and often unidirectional. On one hand, when parents offered suggestions, they may have perceived that the school didn't take them seriously. On the other hand, convinced that teaching was best left to the professionals, the school may have reacted to parents' suggestions as an attempt to "take over." With both society and the family undergoing major changes, families and schools can no longer afford the dubious luxury of considering themselves "separate but equal." Each needs the other in partnership. Stresses on the family have never been greater. In most families, both parents work. Many children are being raised by single parents, or by grandparents. There are more "blended" families.

Schools, too, are under great stress. Although many communities have fewer tax dollars to spend on education, schools are expected to provide additional services such as breakfast programs, health services, and child care both before and after school. These challenges are compounded by the chronic understaffing that many schools experience today.

Society as a whole has undergone large-scale change. Perhaps never before has the United States had to face so many domestic problems at once: an uncertain economy, persistent racism, crime, drug abuse, and inadequate health care, among others. These problems are no longer limited to the cities; they are very much a problem in rural communities as well. To ensure that all children come to school ready to learn, and that schools provide the best possible learning environment, it has become imperative that schools and parents join forces. Collaboration can be difficult to achieve, but schools and parents working together to solve problems can help children become successful learners, both at home and at school. Schools themselves become more effective organizations when they encourage and foster partnerships with parents. In order to build school-family partnerships that support children's learning, many schools are rethinking their parent-involvement practices. For years, parent involvement simply meant that some parents came to Open House, most parents came to parent conferences, and all parents agreed to a tax hike to help pay for the increasing costs of running the school. Activities and events that involved parents, such as the spring play, were conducted annually. For the most part, these activities were based on tradition, rather than on thoughtful planning that considered what the school might need or what parents might really want. Most schools now realize that parent involvement can no longer be something that "happens" in accordance with the calendar. If parents are to become partners with the school, instead of infrequent and uninvolved visitors,

78

educators must initiate efforts to involve parents in new and more meaningful ways.

Rethinking parent involvement means, in part, paying careful attention to who becomes involved, why they become involved, and how to reach the parents who don't usually become involved. It also means redefining what schools mean by parent involvement. Parent involvement is more than parent volunteers and Open House. Parent involvement entails a recognition that parents are a child's first teacher and that schools can help families create home environments that support learning. Parent involvement requires the development of more effective ways to communicate with parents. It means reaching out to parents who are unwilling, reluctant, or unable to visit the school by meeting with them in their own neighborhood or home. Parent involvement recognizes the contributions that parents can make as volunteers and supporters of school activities. It also recognizes parents as contributors to, and resources for, the school. Parent involvement is about parents helping their children at home, and how schools can assist and support that effort. Parent involvement is also about providing parents with the opportunity to develop skills in planning and decision making, and then putting those skills to work in the school.

## ELEMENTS OF EFFECTIVE PRACTICE

Successful parent-involvement programs share several key features. Any one of these alone will not guarantee a successful home-school partnership. But as more of these features become present, the likelihood increases that the program will be meaningful and productive, and that a partnership will develop and grow. These elements include: 1) commitment, collaboration, and communication among the key players; 2) staff and parent training; and 3) comprehensive planning.

### Get Key Players to Buy In

The following guidelines help foster commitment,

collaboration, and communication among administrators, teachers, and parents.

*Provide school board and district-level support.* On one hand, mandating parent involvement is no guarantee that parents will become involved with their child's school, or with their child's education. On the other hand, a clearly defined and articulated policy on parent involvement can encourage the development of programs designed to involve parents in their child's learning. A policy encouraging parent participation and involvement, a clear indication of what is expected and what is valued, and the willingness to provide the resources to do what is needed can provide a foundation upon which to build a parent-involvement program.

An example of school-board and district-level support is provided by the McAllen Parental Involvement Program, McAllen, Texas. Operated by the school district, the program consists of three activities to help parents improve their parenting skills: workshops that use STEPS (Systematic Training for Effective Parenting) and its Spanish version (PECES) to strengthen parenting skills; Evening Study Centers for students at risk and their parents; and group meetings of parents to discuss a variety of topics, such as health and child development.

*Commit administrative support.* Committed leadership by principals helps build trust between parents and schools. The principal leads by example, setting the tone and creating an atmosphere of mutual respect, understanding, and problem solving. When principals openly invite parents into the school and encourage them to be actively involved in a variety of ways, parents receive a message that their presence is welcomed and valued.

For example, because of the high degree of parent involvement at Spring Glen Elementary School, located near Seattle, and the number of parents at the school at any given time, the principal set aside a lounge where parents can plan, share, and store supplies for parent-sponsored activities.

Administrators also have a role in encouraging and assisting teachers in their efforts to involve parents, whether these efforts involve developing a parent workshop, initiating a volunteer program, or producing a class or school newsletter.

An important part of an administrator's role might involve helping teachers improve their communication with parents or develop new ways of communicating. Principals should provide teachers with whatever resources and tools are needed to improve parent involvement, and they should communicate high expectations for parent-school collaboration. They also should make sure to reward teachers' successful efforts to build partnerships with parents.

*Enhance teacher commitment and communication.* Because teachers control the flow of information between home and school, they are perhaps uniquely positioned to help parents feel informed about their child as a student and about the school. Frequent, positive communication also helps parents and teachers get to know each other. With a solid foundation of good communication, teachers and parents are better able to work as partners.

Schools need to communicate with parents often, and in a variety of ways. Newsletters, notes sent home, and open houses are the most common means of establishing communication. Although these are important, it is necessary to develop additional ways for parents and schools to engage in productive dialogue. Phone calls, parent breakfasts, open forums, and parent workshops can spark discussion and serve as tools for encouraging parents' involvement in schools and in their children's education.

For example, at Lake George Elementary School, Lake George, New York, the principal schedules parent-teacher conferences in November after students' first progress report. While parents participate in the evening conference, students and younger children participate in activities organized and supervised by the principal and Parent-Teacher Association members. According to the principal, 99 percent of the parents attend. Parents are also informed of school activities through newspaper articles, a monthly newsletter, and a monthly menu. The school newsletter contains a tear-out section for parents on which they are encouraged to write comments and questions about the newsletter and school programs.

Another example of enhanced communication is Travis Heights Elementary School, Austin, Texas, which initiated an Open Forum Series during the 1992–93 school year. After the first session, the facilitator wrote the following report.

We held our first "Open Forum" tonight at Travis Heights. I was pleased with the way things went. Twenty-five parents showed up, spoke up, and signed up for another session next week! The principal made a few brief introductory remarks, and I facilitated. Since it was our first meeting, I started by suggesting some ground rules and inviting others to add to and/or object to whichever ones they had problems with. We agreed to a nice starter list, including "bring a friend next time" and "share any books, articles, etc., with others in the group between now and the next time, bring them along, or add them to the parent info center." We also agreed to listen carefully to everyone, brainstorm without editorials, have a timekeeper, and stop after an hour and 15 minutes to wrap up, and then wrap up in 15. Then things got underway with a brainstorming session aimed at forming an agenda. I recorded as people offered their concerns, questions, and topics they wanted to discuss.

After a number of questions and concerns were listed, we decided to take on the new progress report first, because there were quite a few related to that, and there was good discussion, good questions, plenty of interest! We did stick to our schedule, though, thanks to a parent timekeeper, and agreed to meet next week (one guy wanted to come back tomorrow night!) when we'll hit the ground running, having our list ready and waiting (Kris Asthalter, NEA School Renewal Network, 1993).

*Ensure parent comfort.* School personnel—principals, teachers, staff, custodians, secretaries, cafeteria workers, and others—all have a role in welcoming parents and other visitors to the school. A friendly smile and a warm hello can put parents at ease. When parents feel welcome in the school, they feel better about themselves and their children.

But what of the building itself? What "signals" does the building send about excluding parents or inviting them in? Is parking convenient? Is the entrance marked? Are there signs directing visitors to the office and other parts of the building? Is students' work prominently displayed? Is there a family center or resource room?

Some schools fail to appreciate the impact these "signals" can have on parents and others who visit the school. Creating a positive, welcoming atmosphere helps to convey the message that "parents are welcome here."

## *Provide Opportunities for Staff and Parent Learning*

Many schools are moving toward more participatory decision-making structures such as site-based management. This requires the development of new skills and new ways of working together. Collaboration, leadership, and communication skills are needed to help teachers and administrators work with parents more effectively. Staff development is a key ingredient in helping to build these cooperative skills.

Some schools have found it helpful to include parents in staff development. They have discovered that parents become more knowledgeable and more supportive of school programs, curriculum, and instruction issues when they are a part of training sessions. Issues that affect both teachers and parents, such as homework and discipline, are often appropriate topics for workshop sessions. Involving parents in training allows teachers and parents to establish a common understanding that can help them work together more effectively.

Parent-teacher conferences are often a cause of anxiety. By skillfully preparing parents, through workshops or written materials, schools can increase the number of parents participating as well as improve the quality of the conferences themselves.

Special learning opportunities that focus on parent-identified needs, scheduled at times that are convenient for parents, provide an effective means of developing skills and supplying information that parents can use to help their children. Many such opportunities can involve teachers, parents, and children in working together, such as Family Math and Family Science workshops. (See resource list at end of book.)

Schools may design their own parent-learning sessions, with teachers, parents, and community members serving as leaders. For example, at Lassiter Middle School, Louisville, Kentucky, the assistant principal initiated "Parent at Lassiter" workshops. Conducted in the evening, these sessions cover topics of concern to middle school parents, teachers, and students. One workshop, on drug abuse, focused on causes, prevention, and intervention, with an emphasis on how parents can help prevent their children from becoming involved with drugs. Community members are frequently invited as guest speakers. For instance, the director of a local treatment center for youth with drug problems led a workshop on drug abuse. At Overbrook Elementary School in Charleston, West Virginia, parents participate in "Parent University," conducted one evening during the first week of school. Overbrook teachers, central office staff, and volunteers from the community lead classes on computers, latchkey safety, child development, and eight other topics. Parents may choose three 20-minute sessions.

### Engage Parents as Partners and Collaborators in the Educational Process

Collaboration is sometimes difficult to achieve within role groups, but it can be even more difficult when the traditional "boundaries" of role groups are crossed. A group may feel threatened by what it perceives as a loss of power. However, when implemented effectively, collaboration can help role groups feel more empowered. The collective will and brainpower of two or more groups can create more lasting and satisfying solutions, with the consultative process ensuring a greater buy-in by all group members.

The following description illustrates how the Family School in Cedar Rapids, Iowa, has engaged parents as partners. The benefit, for teachers, is extra planning time.

My two children, grades three and four, are enrolled in the Family School's program in the district. It consists of approximately 100 students in four multi-aged classrooms (one grades one and two, one grades two and three, one grades three through five, and one grades four and five). The four teachers work to develop thematic, multidisciplinary units that provide a degree of flexibility in learning and instruction.

To give the teachers some additional time for planning, the parents plan an afternoon "Maxi-Lab" or a number of "Mini-Labs" once a quarter. The Maxi-Lab last week consisted of an afternoon of swimming at the Recreation Commission's indoor pool. My wife, (like myself) one of the other teachers at Metro High School (who also has a son in Family School), and I organized drivers, car assignments and supervision, and collected permission slips and money for the activity. Besides being "just plain fun," we hope the event promoted physical activity and social skills, and made a positive connection between the school and the Recreation Commission.

Mini-Labs generally give the students approximately 10 options from which to choose. There have been trips to the art museum, nature center, radio and television stations, local colleges and businesses, and so on. Other parents have taught small groups of students a variety of crafts.

Parents can become involved to the extent that they feel comfortable. Some are willing to organize the entire afternoon, some are willing to teach small groups of students, and some are willing to drive for the activities.

I think the program serves a number of purposes. It provides teachers with additional planning time. It involves parents with the school and, at the same time, offers them a chance to meet and interact with each other. The program also allows parents to use their talents and skills with children. And, it makes students aware of some of the opportunities within the city (Don Daws, Metro High School, NEA School Renewal Network, 1992)

## Develop Meaningful, Comprehensive Plans for Parent Involvement

Comprehensive planning is one of the most critical elements of parent involvement, yet it is often the most overlooked. Schools tend to rely on what they have done in past years without rethinking what they are doing and why. Some of these "old traditions," such as spaghetti dinners and Open House, no longer work as well as they once did. Parents do not want to attend unimportant meetings or participate in activities that they don't find meaningful. Parents want to feel that their time has been well spent.

Schools cannot wait for parents to come to them. Schools need to reach out to all parents, not just those who tend to be highly involved. Educators must learn how to engage parents in new and meaningful partnerships for learning. They must develop a comprehensive, well-organized, and continuing plan for parent involvement at school and at home that:

- allows sufficient planning time
- attends to the needs of both the school and the students
- respects what parents want, not necessarily what teachers think parents want
- provides a balanced, comprehensive program with varied activities that allows for differences in skills and abilities and provides growth opportunities
- encourages teachers, parents, and administrators to work collaboratively.

86

Meaningful planning is best achieved when school staff and parent representatives work together. Chrispeels, Fernandez, and Preston (1990) of San Diego City Schools suggest that a task force of 10 to 15 people, including teachers, support staff, parents, community members, and students (at the secondary level) follow a four-step comprehensive planning process.

1. *Analyzing/Assessing Current Programs:* This includes listing current activities, identifying new ones, and conducting parent/community surveys of attitudes and interests.

2. *Visioning/Action Planning:* This step includes creating a vision/mission statement that defines what you want your parent-school partnership program to be; developing a parent-involvement policy; preparing a plan that contains goals, strategies, and activities; determining responsibilities for implementation; and determining what resources are needed for successful implementation of parent-involvement activities.

3. *Implementation:* This phase entails aiming programs at different audiences (e.g., working parents, single parents, non-English-speaking parents); getting school staff involved; setting and meeting time lines; publicizing and recognizing parent activities.

4. *Evaluation.* The fourth and final phase requires listening to what is being said and conducting surveys to determine how people are reacting to the activities and communications. You must then react to the feedback and use it to improve next year's program.

## CONCLUSION

Schools and families can no longer remain "separate but equal" if they are to solve the complex problems facing children today. Schools must become family places where parents are involved in many aspects of school life. Homes, too, must become centers of learning for children and their parents. Working together, schools and families can create a partnership of support for children that recognizes and depends on the positive influences of each partner. The following poem by an unknown author depicts the interdependence of teachers and parents in their efforts to create successful children.

UNITY
I dreamed I stood in a studio
And watched two sculptors there.
The clay they used was a young child's mind
And they fashioned it with care.
One was a teacher—the tools he used
Were books, music, and art.
The other, a parent, worked with a guiding hand,
And a gentle heart.
Day after day, the teacher toiled with touch
That was deft and sure,
While the parent labored by his side
And polished and smoothed it o'er.
And when at last, their task was done
They were proud of what they had wrought,
For the things they had molded into the child
Could neither be sold nor bought.
And each agreed they would have failed
If each had worked alone.
For behind the teacher stood the school
And behind the parent, the home.

## REFERENCES

Chrispeels, J., Fernandez, B., and Preston, J. 1990. *Home and School: Partners in Student Success.* San Diego, Calif.: San Diego City Schools.

Lezotte, L. Foreword. 1985. In *Beyond the Bake Sale: An Educator's Guide to Working with Parents,* by A. Henderson, C. Marburger, and T. Ooms. Columbia, Md.: National Committee for Citizens in Education.

National Education Association School Renewal Network. 1992, 1993. Participants' comments. Unpublished network content.

# RESOURCES FOR PARENT INVOLVEMENT

Compiled by Barbara A. Fleming

## PRINTED MATERIALS

Albert, L. 1985. *Coping with Kids and School: A Guide for Parents.* New York: Ballantine.

Arizona Department of Education. 1986. *Parent Participation for Effective Schools: Parent Teacher Communication.* Phoenix, Ariz.: Author.

Armistead, L. 1981. *Building Confidence in Education: A Practical Approach for Principals.* Reston, Va.: National Association of Secondary School Principals.

Barth, R. 1990. *Improving Schools from Within: Teachers, Parents, and Principals Can Make the Difference.* San Francisco: Jossey-Bass.

Berger, E. H. 1987. *Parents as Partners in Education,* 2nd edition. Columbus, Ohio: Merrill.

Berla, N., Henderson, A. T., and Kerewsky, W. 1989. *The Middle School Years: A Parents' Handbook.* Washington, D.C.: National Committee for Citizens in Education.

Canter, L., and Canter, M. 1991. *Parents on Your Side: A Comprehensive Parent Involvement Program for Teachers.* Santa Monica, Calif.: Lee Canter and Associates.

Canter, L., and Canter, M. 1991. *Parents on Your Side: Resource Material Workbook.* Santa Monica, Calif.: Lee Canter and Associates.

Canter, L., with Schadlow, B. 1984. *Parent Conference Book.*

Santa Monica, Calif.: Lee Canter and Associates.

Chavkin, N. F., ed. 1993. *Families and Schools in a Pluralistic Society.* Albany, N.Y.: State University of New York Press.

Chrispeels, J., Boruta, M., and Daugherty, M. 1988. *Communicating with Parents.* San Diego, Calif.: San Diego County Office of Education.

Chrispeels, J., Fernandez, B., and Preston, J. 1990. *Partners for Student Success: A Handbook for Principals.* San Diego, Calif.: San Diego City Schools.

Comer, J. 1980. *School Power: Implications of an Intervention Project.* New York: Free Press.

Comer, J. 1989. *Maggie's Dream.* New York: Plume.

Cutright, M. J. 1989. *The National PTA Talks to Parents: How to Get the Best Education for Your Child.* New York: Doubleday in association with the National Parent Teacher Association, 1989.

Decker, L. E., and Decker, V. 1988. *Home/School/Community Involvement.* Arlington, Va.: American Association of School Administrators.

Dinkmeyer, D., and McKay, G. D. 1984. *The Parents' Guide: The STEP Approach for Parenting Your Teen.* New York: Random House.

Dinkmeyer, D., and McKay, G. D. 1989. *Systematic Training for Effective Parenting.* New York: Random House.

Epstein, J. L., and Salinas, K. C. 1993. *School and Family Partnerships: Surveys and Summaries.* Baltimore, Md.: The Johns Hopkins University, Center on Families, Communities, Schools, and Children's Learning.

Epstein, J. L., Conners, L. T., and Salinas, K. C. 1993. *High*

*School and Family Partnerships.* Baltimore, Md.: The Johns Hopkins University, Center on Families, Communities, Schools, and Children's Learning.

Faber, A., and Mazlish, E. 1982. *How to Talk So Kids Will Listen and Listen So Kids Will Talk.* New York: Avon Books.

Ferguson, S., and Mazin, L. E. 1989. *Parent Power.* New York: Clarkson N. Potter.

Garlington, J. A. 1991. *Helping Dreams Survive: The Story of a Project Involving African-American Families in the Education of Their Children.* Washington, D.C.: National Committee for Citizens in Education.

Gordon, T. 1976. *P.E.T. in Action.* New York: Peter H. Wyden.

Gordon, T. 1988. *P.E.T.—Parent Effectiveness Training: The Tested Way to Raise Responsible Children.* New York: New American Library.

Gotts, E. E., and Purnell, R. F. 1985. *Improving Home-School Relations* (Phi Delta Kappa Fastback No. 230). Bloomington, Ind.: Phi Delta Kappa Educational Foundation.

Hansen, B. J., and Marburger, C. L. 1988. *School-Based Improvement: A Manual for District Leaders.* Columbia, Md.: National Committee for Citizens in Education.

Hansen, B. J., and Marburger, C. L. 1989. *School-Based Improvement: A Manual for Training School Councils.* Columbia, Md.: National Committee for Citizens in Education.

Harry, B. 1992. *Cultural Diversity, Families, and the Special Education System.* New York: Teachers College Press.

Henderson, A., and Marburger, C. 1990. *A Workbook on Parent Involvement for District Leaders.* Columbia, Md.: National Committee for Citizens in Education.

Henderson, A., Marburger, C., and Ooms, T. 1985. *Beyond the Bake Sale: An Educator's Guide to Working with Parents.* Columbia, Md.: National Committee for Citizens in Education.

James, B. H. 1988. *Parent Involvement: Asking the Real Questions: Urban Educational Annual Report.* Charleston, W.Va.: Appalachia Educational Laboratory.

Johnson, H. 1990. *The New American Family and the School.* Columbus, Ohio: National Middle School Association.

Krasnow, J. 1990. *Building Parent-Teacher Partnerships: Prospects from the Perspective of the Schools Reaching Out Project.* Boston: Institute for Responsive Education.

Lawrence, G., and Hunter, M. 1978. *Parent-Teacher Conferencing.* El Segundo, Calif.: TIP Publications.

Liontos, L. B. 1992. *At-Risk Families and Schools: Becoming Partners.* Eugene, Ore.: ERIC Clearinghouse on Educational Management.

Lyons, P., Robbins, A., and Smith, A. 1982. *Involving Parents: A Handbook for Participation in Schools.* Ypsilanti, Mich.: High/Scope Press.

Maeroff, G. 1989. *The School Smart Parent: A Guide for Knowing What Your Child Should Know—From Infancy Through the End of Elementary School.* New York: Times Books.

McAfee, O. 1984. *Improving School-Home Communications: A Resource Notebook for Staff Developers.* Charleston, W.Va.: Appalachia Education Laboratory.

Meyers, J. W. 1989. *Involving Parents in Middle Level Education.* Columbus, Ohio: National Middle School Association.

Meyers, J. W., and Monson, L. 1992. *Involving Families.* Columbus, Ohio: National Middle School Association.

National Committee for Citizens in Education. 1984. *Finding Out How People Feel About Local Schools.* Columbia, Md.: Author.

Oakes, J., and Lipton, M. 1990. *Making the Best of Schools: A Handbook for Parents, Teachers, and Policymakers.* New Haven, Conn.: Yale University Press.

Perroncel, C. B. 1993. *Parent Involvement: An Essential Element for Student Success* (policy background paper for reauthorization of the Elementary and Secondary Education Act). Charleston, W.Va.: Appalachia Educational Laboratory.

Rich, D. 1988. *MegaSkills: How Families Can Help Children Succeed in School and Beyond.* Boston: Houghton Mifflin.

Rutherford, R. B., Jr., and Edgar, E. 1979. *Teachers and Parents: A Guide to Interaction and Cooperation.* Boston: Allyn and Bacon.

Sattes, B. D. 1985. *Parent Involvement: A Review of the Literature.* Charleston, W.Va.: Appalachia Education Laboratory.

Sattes, B. D. 1986. *Parent Involvement: Improving School-Family Communications and Effective Parent-School Relationships.* Charleston, W.Va.: Appalachia Education Laboratory.

Saunders, H. V. 1990. *School Advisory Councils: How to Get Everyone on Board the Same Train . . . On the Same Track . . .*

*Going in the Same Direction.* Charleston, W.Va.: West Virginia Association of School Administrators in association with Appalachia Educational Laboratory.

Saunders, H. V. 1990. *Why Parent Involvement?* Charleston, W.Va.: West Virginia Association of School Administrators in association with Appalachia Educational Laboratory.

Shoemaker, J. 1984. *Research-Based School Improvement Practices* Hartford, Conn.: Connecticut State Department of Education.

Stenmark, J. K., Thompson, V., and Cossey, R. 1986. *Family Math.* Berkeley, Calif.: Lawrence Hall of Science, University of California at Berkeley.

Swap, S. M. 1984. *Enhancing Parent Involvement in Schools.* New York: Teachers College Press.

Swap, S. M. 1990. *Parent Involvement and Success for All Children: What We Know Now.* Boston: Institute for Responsive Education.

Swap, S. M., and Braun, L. A. 1987. *Building Parent Home-School Partnerships: An Instructional Kit.* Boston: Wheelock College.

Wikelund, K. R. 1990. *Schools and Communities Together: A Guide to Parent Involvement.* Portland, Ore.: Northwest Regional Educational Laboratory.

Williams, D. L., Jr., and Chavkin, N. F. 1985. *Teacher/Parent Partnerships: Guidelines and Strategies for Training Teachers in Parent Involvement Skills.* Austin, Tex.: Southwest Educational Development Laboratory.

## MEDIA-BASED PARENTING RESOURCES

*Active Parenting* and *Active Parenting of Teens.* Video-based workshops. Active Parenting Publishers, 810 Franklin Ct., Ste. B, Marietta, GA 30067 (ph. 800/825-0060).

*Assertive Discipline for Parents, Homework Without Tears,* and *Parent Involvement Program.* Videotapes. Lee Canter and Associates, Inc., P.O. Box 2113, Santa Monica, CA 90406 (ph. 800/262-4347 or 213/395-3221). Workshops and video-based workshop kits are also available.

*How to Talk So Kids Will Listen and Listen So Kids Will Talk.* Videotape. Negotiation Institute, Inc., 230 Park Avenue, New York, NY 10169 (ph. 212/986-5555). Workshops and video-based workshop kits are also available.

*STEP: Systematic Training for Effective Parenting.* Videotape. American Guidance Service, P.O. Box 99, Circle Pines, MN 55014-1796 (ph. 800/247-5053). Workshops and video-based workshop kits are also available.

*Success in Schools Is Homemade,* a free parent-involvement resource kit developed by the Missouri Department of Education. Contact Jim Morris, Director of Public Information, Missouri Department of Education, P.O. Box 480, Jefferson City, MO 65102 (ph. 314/751-3469).


## PARENT WORKSHOPS

*Family Connections.* Appalachia Educational Laboratory, P.O. Box 1348, Charleston, WV 25325 (ph. 304/347-0400). Set of 30 four-page guides to help families help their young children learn.

*Family Math.* Lawrence Hall of Science, University of California at Berkeley, Berkeley, CA 94720 (ph. 415/642-1823). Workshops are available.

*Family Science.* Northwest Equals, Portland State University, P.O. Box 1491, Portland OR 97207-1491 (ph. 800/547-8887). Workshops are available.

*MegaSkills Leader Training.* MegaSkills Education Center, Home and School Institute, 1500 Massachusetts Ave., N.W., Washington, DC 20005 (ph. 202/466-3633). Workshops for parent and classroom programs available.

*TIPS* (Teachers Involve Parents in Schoolwork). School and Family Connections Project, Johns Hopkins University, 3505 N. Charles St., Baltimore, MD 21218. Program helps teachers more effectively involve parents in their child's schoolwork. Modules include science, mathematics, social studies, and art.

## HELPFUL ORGANIZATIONS

American Association of School Administrators, 1801 N. Moore St., Arlington, VA 22209-9988 (ph. 703/875-0703.

American Federation of Teachers, 11 Dupont Circle, Washington, DC 20036 (ph. 202/797-4494).

Appalachia Educational Laboratory, PO Box 1348, Charleston, WV 25325 (ph. 304/347-0400).

ASPIRA Association, Inc., National Office, 1112 16th St., NW, Ste. 340, Washington, DC 20036 (ph. 202/835-3600).

Association for Supervision and Curriculum Development, 1250 N. Pitt St. Alexandria, VA 22314-1403 (ph. 703/549-9110).

Center for Early Adolescence, University of North Carolina at Chapel Hill, Ste. 223, Carr Mill Mall, Carrboro, NC 27510 (ph. 919/966-1148).

Center on Parent Involvement, Center for Social Organization of Schools, Johns Hopkins University, 3505 N. Charles St., Baltimore, MD 21218 (ph. 410/338-7570).

Council for Basic Education, 725 15th St., NW, Washington, DC 20005 (ph. 202/347-4171).

Designs for Change, 220 S. State St., Ste. 1900, Chicago, IL 60604 (ph. 312/922-0317).

Family Matters Project, College of Human Ecology, Cornell Distribution Center, 7 Research Park, Cornell University, Ithaca, NY 14850 (ph. 607/255-2080).

Harvard Family Research Project, Harvard University Graduate School of Education, Longfellow Hall, Appian Way, Cambridge, MA 02138 (ph. 617/495-9108).

IMPACT II, The Teachers Network, PO Box 577, Canal St. Station, New York, NY 10013-0577 (ph. 212/966-5582).

Institute for Responsive Education, Boston University, 605 Commonwealth Ave., Boston, MA 02215 (ph. 617/353-3309).

Intercultural Development Research Association, 5835 Callaghan, Ste. 350, San Antonio, TX 78228 (ph. 512/684-8180).

Marcus Foster Institute, 1203 Preservation Parkway, Suite 300, Oakland, CA 94612 (ph. 510/835-0391).

MegaSkills Education Center, 1500 Massachusetts Ave., NW, Washington, DC 20005 (ph. 202/466-3633).

Methods for Achieving Parent Partnerships (MAPP), Indianapolis Public Schools, 901 North Carrolton, Indianapolis, IN 40202 (ph. 317/266-4134).

National Association of Elementary School Principals, 1615 Duke St., Alexandria, VA 22314 (ph. 703/684-3345).

National Association of Partners in Education, Inc., 601 Wythe St., Ste. 200 Alexandria, VA 22314 (ph. 703/836-4880).

National Association of Secondary School Principals, 1904 Association Dr., Reston, VA 22091 (ph. 703/860-0200).

National Black Child Development Institute (NBCDI), 1463 Rhode Island Ave., NW, Washington, DC 20005 (ph. 202/387-1281).

National Coalition of Title I/Chapter I Parents, National Parent Center, 1314 14th St., NW, Washington, DC 20005 (ph. 202/483-8822).

National Committee for Citizens in Education, 900 2nd St., NE, Ste. 8, Washington, DC 20002-4307 (ph. 202/408-0447).

National Congress of Parents and Teachers (PTA), 700 N. Rush St., Chicago, IL 60611 (ph. 312/787-0977).

National Council of La Raza, 20 F St., NW, Washington, DC 20001 (ph. 202/628-9600).

National Education Association, 1201 16th St., NW, Washington, DC 20036-3290 (ph. 202/822-7000).

National Middle School Association, 4807 Evanswood Dr., Columbus, OH 43229 (ph. 614/848-8211).

National Research Center on Families, Communities, and Children's Learning, Boston University, 605

Commonwealth Ave., Boston, MA 02215 (ph. 617/353-3309).

National School Boards Association, 1680 Duke St., Alexandria, VA 22314 (ph. 703/838-6722).

National Urban Coalition, 1120 G St., NW, Ste. 900, Washington, DC 20005 (ph. 202/628-2988).

National Urban League, Inc., 500 E. 62d St., New York, NY 10021 (ph. 212/310-9000).

Parent Outreach Project, 2805 E. 10th St., Ste. 150, Bloomington, IN 47408-2698 (ph. 812/855-5847).

Parents as Teachers Program, PAT National Center School of Education, University of Missouri–St. Louis, 8001 Natural Bridge Rd., Saint Louis, MO 63121 (ph. 314/553-5738).

San Diego City Schools, Parent Involvement Department, 4100 Normal St., Rm. 2109, San Diego, CA 92103 (ph. 619/293-8560).

San Diego County Office of Education, 6401 Linda Vista Rd., Rm. 407, San Diego, CA 92111-7399 (ph. 619/569-5391).

School-Age Child Care Project Center for Research on Women, Wellesley College, Wellesley, MA 02181 (ph. 617/431-1453).

School Strategies and Options, PO Box 1705, Lunenberg, MA 01462 (ph. 508/582-4217).

Southwest Educational Development Laboratory, 211 E. 7th St., Austin, TX 78701 (ph. 512/476-6861).

# THE CONTRIBUTORS

*Rebecca Crawford Burns,* M.A., is a research and development specialist at the Appalachia Educational Laboratory in Charleston, West Virginia. A former secondary English teacher and curriculum supervisor, she currently manages an educational research project on interdisciplinary teamed instruction. Burns has experience as a developer and presenter of workshops on parent involvement for parent and educator audiences. She has served as parent-involvement researcher for the NEA School Renewal Network, and currently moderates the Network's Curriculum conference.

*Robert D. Childers,* Ed.D., is director of the Appalachia Educational Laboratory's Rural Excel Program, which produced *Family Connections.* Dr. Childers has been an elementary and secondary school teacher, a school counselor, and a professor of counselor education at Radford University in Radford, Virginia. He was a member of the Education Testing Service team that conducted the initial evaluation of Head Start, and later served as field director of the Home-Oriented Preschool Education (HOPE) program. From 1992-93 he directed a project to assess the effectiveness of the Appalachia Regional Commission/ International Business Machines Writing-to-Read project in a three-state region.

*Clyde Collins,* B.S., is a science teacher at Mynderse Academy in Seneca Falls, NY. He was cochair of the school's Mastery in Learning Project and led the development of a district-wide site-based management model. He currently serves on both the high school and district management teams and is the Mynderse site-based computer coordinator for the NEA School Renewal Network.

*Barbara A. Fleming,* B.S.J., is co-moderator of the Parent and Community Involvement Conference of the NEA School Renewal Network. She and her husband operate School Strategies and Options, a consulting firm that assists schools and districts with planning, problem solving, and team development. Barbara is author of several publications that help parents and community members better understand school development strategies. She also conducts interactive training programs for parents in MegaSkills, Gender/Ethnic Expectations and Student Achievement, and Team Problem-Solving Tools.

*Oralie McAfee,* Ed.D., is professor emeritus at Metropolitan State College of Denver, Colorado, as well as a writer and consultant. Dr. McAfee's publications and workshops on parent involvement are grounded in her practical experience as a parent, teacher, and teacher and parent educator. Her most recent publication, *Assessing and Guiding Young Children's Development and Learning* (Allyn and Bacon 1993), a text for preservice and inservice teachers, includes sections on involving parents in student assessment and communicating with them about assessment.

*Patricia Hamrick Penn,* M.S.J., a staff associate at the Appalachia Educational Laboratory, is writer-editor of *Family Connections.* She has taught high school English and college journalism, and has conducted workshops throughout the United States for human services professionals and educators. Before joining the *Family Connections* project, she was director of continuing medical education and public relations at the West Virginia University School of Medicine, where she edited and published a quarterly magazine, *Outreach.*

*Robert R. Simmons,* Ed.D., is principal of Stewart Community School in Flint, Michigan, and adjunct professor at Eastern Michigan University, where he teaches courses in educational administration and supervision. He is listed in *Who's Who Among American Teachers* (1990) and recently has been nominated for *Who's Who in American Education.*

*Barbara A. Stevenson,* M.A., is an elementary reading teacher at Stewart Community School in Flint, Michigan. A past president of the American Association of University Women, she has been a Chapter 1 consultant and trainer for teachers in the whole language approach for the Flint School District.

*Ann M. Strnad,* M.A., is an elementary Chapter 1 mathematics teacher at Stewart Community School in Flint, Michigan. She serves as cochair of the Stewart Improvement Team under the Flint District Site-Based Management Model and as the site-based computer coordinator for the NEA School Renewal Network. A 1989 Christa McAuliffe Educator, she has been nominated recently for *Who's Who in American Education.*